Why South Sudan Matters

GARANG MALONG

GEMS Development Foundation
Alexandria, VA

Published by
G.E.M.S. Development Foundation
Alexandria, VA
www.goatsfortheoldgoat.com

© 2016 Garang Malong

ISBN: 978-0-69277-673-5

All rights reserved.

All rights reserved. No part of this publication may be reproduced, scanned, uploaded, stored in a retrieval system, or transmitted, in any form or by any means, electronic, mechanical, photocopying, recording, or otherwise, without the prior written permission of the publisher.

Edited by Shari Johnson
Cover & interior by Gary A. Rosenberg

Printed in the United States of America

*To the South Sudanese
orphans and widows of war,
and to the brothers, sisters,
mothers and fathers
that we have lost.*

Contents

Why Should South Sudan Matter?, 1

Prologue, 5

BOOK ONE HEIRS OF FALLEN HEROES

PART I

Chapter 1, 12

Chapter 2, 16

Chapter 3, 19

Chapter 4, 21

Chapter 5, 24

PART II

Chapter 6, 26

Chapter 7, 28

PART III

Chapter 8, 34

Chapter 9, 37

Chapter 10, 44

PART IV

Chapter 11, 47

Chapter 12, 52

Chapter 13, 54

Chapter 14, 60

Chapter 15, 63

Chapter 16, 71

BOOK TWO **THE THEATRE OF HOPE**

Introduction, 78

PART I **A LEGACY OF WAR**

Chapter 1. Background, 82

Chapter 2. Underdevelopment (A British Colonial Legacy), 86

Chapter 3. Education—Not a Priority, 91

Chapter 4. My Father's Story, 96

Chapter 5. Exodus to Ethiopia, 104

Chapter 6. Starting Over in Kenya, 111

PART II **CHILDREN AT WAR**

Chapter 7. The Reprehensible Side of War, 116

Chapter 8. Girls at Greater Risk, 120

Chapter 9. Recruitment of Children, 123

Chapter 10. Can Anything Be Done?, 127

PART III **EDUCATION—THE THEATRE OF HOPE**

Chapter 11. Education *Must* Be the Priority!, 133

Chapter 12. A Sense of Urgency, 144

PART IV **SURVIVING THE WAR**

Chapter 13. Higher Education—No Bed of Roses, 142

Chapter 14. Home to South Sudan, 150

A Debt of Gratitude, 154

BOOK THREE **PATRIOTISM— SOUTH SUDAN, MY COUNTRY**

Acknowledgments, 164

About the Author, 165

Why Should South Sudan Matter?

THE AFRICAN COUNTRY OF SOUTH SUDAN is the world's newest country, gaining independence from Sudan on July 9, 2011. It is strategically located, bordering Ethiopia and Eritrea to the east; Libya, Central African Republic, and Chad to the west; Kenya, Uganda, and Democratic Republic of Congo to the south; Sudan to the north.

South Sudan's population is estimated currently at between 12 and 13 million with a land mass of approximately 385,000 miles.

Our official language is English. South Sudan is a Christian nation, while Sudan is Islamic. Before gaining our independence from Sudan, we fought the north Sudanese for over five decades to maintain our identification as Christian and as black people with a diverse culture. We fought not only for ourselves, but also to save this part of the world from Islamization. Were it not for South Sudan, the whole of East, Central and Southern Africa would now be an Islamic State.

The plan of the Muslims in north Sudan was to make South Sudan its headquarters for terrorism and administer

South Sudan from Khartoum, where they intended to spread their doctrine from the north to the southern parts of Africa. When South Sudan first gained its independence, the offer came to join the Arab League with *opportunities* for economic and political support—the same group that never stood with us when we were for years enslaved by Islamic north Sudan, and in fact stood with the people who were killing us. The leadership and all the communities of South Sudan stood together as one to reject their offer. South Sudan joined the East African Community and is committed to stop the spread of Islam.

However, even as I write this, terrorism is spreading in the north and affecting major cities in East African countries. Somalia is struggling with terror attacks, as are Kenya and Uganda. Do not think that any country on any continent is immune from this plague.

Why is the Islamic State so interested in South Sudan, a country where illiteracy is over 70 percent and thought to be the highest in the world? One word: resources.

South Sudan is rich in vast, largely untapped, natural resources. One of our major resources is the River Nile with its many tributaries running throughout the country. Other resources include oil, iron ore, copper, gold, silver, zinc, chromium ore, tungsten, mica, and hydropower. Our agricultural produce includes cotton, groundnuts (peanuts), sorghum, millet, wheat, sugarcane, cassava (tapioca), mangoes, papaya, bananas, sweet potatoes, and sesame.

We desperately need help in tapping these resources. While other countries were becoming industrial, technological giants, we were trying to stay alive—fighting a war we did not start or even understand. We want to learn, and we want to learn from those who have stood with us, supported us, and believed in us. I don't need to explain what would happen if these resources were to come under the control of the Islamic State.

The country of South Sudan is founded on democracy. Yes, our people are strong and have fought valiantly for over fifty years for independence, but democracy is what won our long-awaited peace. It is well known in South Sudan that this would not have been possible without the support of America. Former President George W. Bush pushed for the introduction of democracy as a means to end the bloodshed. America, Britain and other European countries, Norway and Israel have all supported South Sudanese refugees on humanitarian issues and in many other ways. We cannot stand alone. If these countries leave us, it will ultimately mean the spread of terrorism.

The people of South Sudan have always seen America as a role model. There is a saying in my city of Aweil, "Mading Aweil chit Amerika," which means, "The people of Mading Aweil are like American people." They could not pay a higher compliment than that.

The South Sudanese are friendly, honest people who respect the opinions of others and are true to our word. We are proud of who we are—black people of the Nile valley. For the most part, we have been denied education, but that is the hope for our future. We are hungry to learn. We want to develop a foreign policy. We want to be a positive presence in the world.

We are reaching out to you to partner with us—America, Europe, Norway, Israel, and any democracy that can understand that South Sudan cannot fail. At this point, your world

Why South Sudan Matters

is not our world, and our world is not yours. However, by working together, learning together, and understanding each other, our separate worlds can become one—with one goal, with one desire—peace for our families and for generations yet to come.

Garang Malong Awan

Prologue

THIS BOOK IS A REVISION AND ANTHOLOGY of my three previous books published in Africa. These books are often graphic and disturbing, but there is no other way to tell the story of South Sudan.

Heirs of Fallen Heroes is a composite of thousands of people in South Sudan—both the living and the dead. I narrate the events in this book from personal experience and from the stories told to me by the experiences of others. Dombai, Abuk, and their children Riel and Nhier are a fictional family in names only.

The time line is from 1983 to the present, and although this book relates facts of the many wars and conflicts in my beleaguered country, my intention in writing it is to focus on the children of the forgotten freedom fighters. One can read in newspapers and on the Internet or hear from news broadcasts that a war or conflict has ended somewhere in the world and perhaps feel relieved, happy or even indifferent . . . but the true story does not stop there. For some in those countries there is cause for celebration, but for the immense number of orphans and children, a hard life simply gets harder. Some have no idea what has happened to their parents or if their parents are even still alive. They worry about how they are going to be able to survive in a place where no one cares what happens to them.

The Theatre of Hope is more autobiographical in nature. What an amazing—often tragic—journey it has been. Although it is more comfortable to narrate a true story of fictional characters, this was *my* country, *my* story, *my* life. I stared death in the face countless times, but I was not on this journey alone. Many were the days when a friend died of a bullet wound as we helplessly watched him die; many were the days in the forest and the refugee camp when we nearly starved to death; many were the days when we literally lived one day at a time.

Too many of our number gave up the biggest battle of all—life. We grew up under the most trying circumstances where we survived purely on providence. The wasteful, protracted civil war was a devastating experience that took millions of lives and incapacitated many others, leaving in its wake a shattered country.

In addition, there was the urgency I felt to convey the message that was burning in my heart and mind. The severity of the complexities buffeting South Sudan demanded that they be addressed with the immediacy they deserved, given that I had decided to focus on the single most important propellant in moving my nation forward—education.

We know where we have come from; we know where we are now. We know where we are going and what can be done to avert the crisis that is inexorably intertwined in our fate as a new nation. To me, if we could not rise to the occasion from the outset and learn from the mistakes of other African coun-

Prologue

tries, we were about to take the predictable path that virtually every African country has taken after gaining their independence: political instability, massive debt, economic disaster, depletion of natural resources, and poverty.

Yet our situation was unique. We were struggling to emancipate ourselves, not from European colonial tyranny this time, but from our mother nation that for many years had abused our rights. At the time we became a republic, the illiteracy level in South Sudan was among the highest in the world. Something had to be done.

Poverty levels were startling. The physical infrastructure in the country was woefully inadequate. Schools, hospitals, and other amenities such as recreational facilities were non-existent in many parts of the country. Up to the point of receiving our independence, access to basic utilities such as electricity; clean, piped water; and contemporary means of communication was extremely limited. Things have slightly improved but there is yet a lot of ground to cover.

Despite this, our country is supremely endowed with resources, tremendous cultural diversity and an eager citizenship ready to steer the country into the promising future.

I believe that the future of South Sudan lies in educating its young as well as the older generation, who can then dutifully take up the responsibility of spearheading the destiny of our great country. The Chinese say that if you think education is expensive, try ignorance. Ignorance has been the bane of Africa as a continent and has killed more people than anything else since those highly optimistic times half a century ago when every African believed that with independence and self-governance came a brighter future.

Ignorance has played a huge role in shaping the unenviable situation that Africa as a continent is currently grappling with. Africa still boasts the highest number of illiterate people, mostly due to institutional failure and systemic discrimination that has locked as many children out of school as possible. These children and youth have been used by the merchants of death, wasting their formative years on the battlefield fighting for a cause utterly unknown to them.

These children are also pawns of human traffickers, and are exported to the Middle East, Asia, Europe, and other destinations as a source of cheap labour. In some extreme cases, they are used for more diabolical schemes, such as satisfying the voyeuristic desires of dirty, rich old men. Many young women end up as prostitutes in the Western capitals, yet little or no attention is paid to their plight while the traffickers laugh all the way to the bank.

Our political leaders have failed—their greed has kept them from stopping for even a moment to consider the future of this continent. Also, the African masses have been the recipients of bad policies that have been rammed down our throats from other countries for far too long.

However, it is encouraging that more and more leaders are discovering the folly of their ways and charting the way forward, the nearly insuperable challenges notwithstanding. This has been the case in many warring countries where more peaceful solutions are being sought as the guns are being laid to rest—albeit not fast enough.

Shall one therefore say that the destiny of African countries lies solely in their hands? Arguably, many countries that have moved forward are those that came to this self-realization and embarked on building their nation. Out of sheer hard work, utmost dedication and a sense of purpose, many a great

Prologue

country has been born. But one key aspect of growth as a nation is ensuring that the majority have access to formal education.

Formal education helps wash away prejudice and contributes to the national cohesion of a country. Prejudice is inevitable, but anyone who is sufficiently educated and informed will be more likely to rise above the pettiness of it all. In a country as ethnically, religiously, and culturally diverse as ours, education will certainly be the key to unlock the potential within our country. Tapping into the intrinsic diversity has helped all the developed countries, and more so, the United States. We must do likewise.

Hence, by presenting my story, I believe it can be an instructive tale to the young boy and girl in school and would serve to ignite a desire in them to thirst for knowledge.

Patriotism—South Sudan, My Country is a booklet written to inspire and promote pride and patriotism.

Even after all that the South Sudanese have endured, we are a fiercely patriotic people. Yet the evils of corruption and greed can destroy us or any other nation. We must all be aware and vigilant.

My father once told me, "My soldiers are dying every day; I won't take a chance of leading them into war after war. It is time we had peace in South Sudan." We have since gained independence from Sudan and we continue to enjoy the peace despite the disruptions that keep setting the country backward. There is still more work to be done. We soldier on.

Garang Malong Awan

BOOK ONE

Heirs of Fallen Heroes

PART I

Chapter One

DOMBAI WAS A YOUNG BOY when he learned to fend for his family. The scorching heat for more than half the year made life insufferable in the vast, flat lands of the Bahr el Ghazal zones of South Sudan. In addition, there were the incessant attacks by the northerners that were driving many of his clansmen out of their ancestral land.

Dombai was barely 18 when he married, and by the age of 20, he already had two children. Like many of his clansmen, he was a tall, lanky fellow with smooth, ebony skin the colour of shining obsidian rock. He was humble, modest, and a committed father—a shining example to many young men growing up. He was also a brave man, dedicated to see that people were not expelled from their ancestral land.

The war pitting the Arabs of north Sudan against the largely Christian-animist south escalated, and in recent times the Arabs had developed the despised practice of razing vil-

Chapter One

lages in the south. This was devastating to the villagers. With their houses and food stores burnt, a few went to refugee camps, but many disappeared into the forests, with men joining the guerilla movement and women and children generally getting lost in the process. Some did find their way to a neighbouring country, or anywhere else in the south with a modicum of peace.

Then, at the beginning of the year, one such attack staged by the northerners left in their wake one of the worst famines ever witnessed in that part of the world. The rains were more than six months away. Villagers turned to wild fruits and wild animals for survival. Before this attack, many villagers had abandoned the hunting and gathering culture—but with the burning of their food stores, they had to return to the basics of hunting and gathering. Only a few communities stayed in bushes and forests around the Equatorial region.

After the attack, Dombai was livid with anger. As one of the remaining older men, he began to contemplate ways that could stop the relentless raids from the north. What angered him most was that even the elderly and the sick had been left with no options other than to forage for food themselves. In the past, it was always the young men who went to the forests, but they were now absorbed in the war and the elderly had to kill the wild animals and find the edible wild fruits on their own. And given the current drought, food was scarce.

The village's survival was on the line, so Dombai thought quickly and mobilised several young men to form an army that would protect their livestock and the community at large. They called the unit Gel Weng, which means *protect the cattle*. Their efforts were thwarted again and again as the northerners raided more ferociously, and with heightened frequency. They persistently burnt down the huts and stores and took the cattle. They knew very well that the villagers' livestock was the mainstay of the economy and the lifeblood of the villagers. In fact, livestock was and still is everything to the Dinka community and several other tribes in the south, as it is to nearly all pastoralist communities in Africa. A family may have several thousand bags of sorghum, but if they do not have cattle, they are deemed poor.

Gel Weng was a relatively small unit that directed their energies to protect the community and its livestock. Therefore, members of Gel Weng became the community's warriors. While the northerners had more sophisticated weaponry, the Gel Weng used spears and traps to kill the enemies in the same way they hunted animals.

No sooner had the raiders burnt down the village than the villagers rebuilt the houses. This had been the way of life since Sudan obtained its independence in 1956 from the joint Egyptian and British government that administrated Sudan. It degenerated into a game of hide and seek that pitted the northern government troops against the poor community of Dinka Malual. However, the Gel Weng was trained to fight and it offered the community a chance to escape from the menacing guns and bombs of the enemy. It became an ongoing cat and mouse game that lasted over a span of many years.

The community had two options: turn into rebels or convert to Islam. Rebellion was a better option, considering that even if a person converted to Islam it would not necessarily shield him wholly from other forms of oppression. The cat and mouse game empowered the Gel Weng's resolve and they actually did succeed in killing a number of the government troops and stealing their guns and other weapons from time

Chapter One

to time. [*This is what led to the formation of the AnyaNya I, a southern Sudanese rebel army.*] While still no match for the government troops, the Gel Weng were sufficiently armed to take on the government fighters. The government troops were increasingly caught unawares; given that in previous years rarely were Dombai's men a threat. The cat was no longer aware that the mouse was better armed and, as such, was better able to defend itself. The mouse even threatened to defeat the cat from time to time. Many of the northerners were killed, some were wounded, and more ran away. The wounded were tortured and killed by the community members who returned from their hideouts when they could hear no more gunshots. This is what brought peace to the village —even though it was temporary.

People resumed their daytime businesses at Warawar, and some of the businesses boomed—all due to the resilience of the people of Bahr el Ghazal.

Chapter Two

IN THE ENSUING PEACEFUL TIMES, Dombai opened a hardware store in the market for his wife, Abuk. His two children, a son named Riel and a daughter named Nhier, were still young and he would take them on picnics, buy them candy, and play with them when he was not at his law office, where he was a legal officer in the court. The son, though young, was growing fast and quickly taking after the father—taller than most boys his age, athletic and tough, but humble. He rarely fought with other boys, but none of his peers would face him in a fight. Anytime his friends fought, he would speedily mediate, restoring order in admirable fashion. There were many such feuds, and it took Riel to call them to order. As for his sister, Nhier was quiet and calm, never loud and shouting as her friends did.

Dombai was the model family man. To the delight of his dutiful wife, he was a loving provider and protector. This made Abuk the envy of other wives who had married less committed men. Everything was going quite as Abuk expected (or as most women wish it to be when they marry and have children). However, she worried that Dombai, being every woman's dream husband, might be swayed to marry a younger, second wife, as that was the tradition.

Chapter Two

Although this was all in her imagination, it was understandable that she would have such fears. Her own father had three wives, her mother being the third and the youngest wife. Therefore, according to the code of the community, Abuk's desire to be the only wife to Dombai would have branded her as selfish if she ever voiced her fears.

Although he had never travelled out of Sudan, Dombai possessed a rare business acumen by the entire region's standards. He was a fierce proponent of business between and among different clans and communities. He fervently discouraged clan wars that became common when the raids from the north were less frequent. In the mornings he worked in his law office as a legal officer; in the afternoons he helped his wife in their hardware store; and in the evenings as the sun set, he went to his farm to tend to it. In contrast, most of the other men in the village had little concern for their families, and in fact left many responsibilities to their wives. Occasionally they would be seen shopping in the village market, or watching community football or wrestling at the communal *riangkou*. [*A field, or in this case it was more like a modified stadium.*]

In his brief interactions with white men who had once visited and even lived in Warawar, he had learned distinguished European traditions. Some in the village considered him an English gentleman, given his strict following of routines (that the more cynical types labeled pretentious). For instance, his evening routine became something of a curiosity to the villagers. Dombai would buy mangoes and oranges for his two children and take them for a walk. After that he would take his family for dinner, sometimes in the hotels in Warawar. Come eight o'clock it was always story time, before the kids would go to sleep. Not many men had the attachment to their families that Dombai did. Many assumed that by fighting in the war, it absolved them of any duty and responsibilities. Therefore, many of the households were run by women.

In the ensuing peaceful days, especially if the rains had been sufficient, villagers would revel in their harvest, which they would trade during the open market days. The farmers were often rewarded for their patience and hard work. This was followed by sacrifices to gods during ceremonies, such as weddings. Riel used to sit next to his father whenever they went to court or to the market. It was a sign of the freedom of the times, given that in the past the children were usually in the company of their mothers, hiding in forests while their fathers fought. Other signs of freedom, although not as positive, were the drunkards sleeping by the roadside and the large number of night runners and thieves who ran amok through the whole village at night. This had not happened in Warawar in a long time.

Chapter Three

DOMBAI'S HARDWARE BUSINESS WAS DOING WELL. He was the village's chief supplier of iron sheets and other building material, and was solely responsible for the booming construction enterprise in the village. Stately houses were built. Dombai built an impressive one for his own family that was the envy of the villagers. While he was building the house, his precocious son took over the family business in Warawar. Most weekends the family traveled to scenic places and explored nature's beauty in the expansive, largely virgin parts of the predominantly flat land of Sudan. On other days, father and son would go on hunting expeditions. Sometimes they would go swimming in any of the opulent hotels in Awiel, the state's capital. As early as the age of five, Riel had demonstrated that he was interested in succeeding his father in his business interests. As soon as he came from school, he would go to the farm to help his father or follow him to the family store where he would compel his father to help him with his homework.

Several peaceful months had gone by without any attack or sign of attack from the north. Their rebellion against the northerners had paid huge dividends. Everyone was enjoying peace. Schoolchildren were now encouraged never to miss school, when before it was not considered very important. Riel also wanted to be a lawyer like his father. Education was going to be the single most important liberator of the masses from the tyranny of the north. [*Later, when the airstrip in Malualkon was built, it would inspire most pupils to be pilots and engineers.*]

Chapter Four

DOMBAI'S LIFE ROTATED AROUND HIS FAMILY, the hardware store, his law firm, and farming, which was seasonal. At Warawar, the Sultan was counting his blessings. Never, since before the arrival of the British Missionaries and the subsequent colonization, had they enjoyed peace over a longer period than now. For the time being, there were no threats, the possibility of attacks, or any fear of a raid. [*The last war involved artillery.*] With the climate of peace and business booming, both petty and grievous crimes went down, doubly affecting Dombai's legal work at Warawar. As the days went by, Dombai trusted his manager with much of the work in the office, and would receive a report from him in the evening. He preferred spending his time with his children.

However, as many adults knew, the peaceful period was not going to last. Many waited for the *surprise*. Some even desired it. The village madman once quipped, "I survived well under threats and tension." Unfortunately, his wish was granted, and a few days later all hell broke loose. The devil returned with a vengeance. In the days before the attack, there was a cloud of lingering smoke that was a sure sign of a smouldering fire that would erupt soon.

On the night they struck, the northern Bahr el Ghazal

chairperson of SPLA/M [*Sudan People's Liberation Army/ Movement*], General Paul Malong, came to Dombai's house. When Dombai opened the door, they shook hands. General Malong apologised and said, "Sorry that I have to wake you up at this time, comrade Dombai, but we need you. You must call up your young men, the Gel Weng. The enemy is upon us. What we must not allow is for them to fight us on our grounds. That will harm our families."

"Okay, General," Dombai replied. He went back to his room and dressed in his beige khaki pants. His wife was in bed, oblivious of what was happening—or about to happen. She was probably half-asleep, assuming that Dombai was going to see to the children or the cattle and be right back. She turned away, shrugging in protest from the flicker of light from the torch. He switched off the torch and walked out.

He went about knocking on every door in Warawar, and after a few minutes they were all gathered in Dombai's compound. The men had been trained to be always alert and on the ready. They were young and energetic. Dombai said, "Gentlemen, I know it is late to wake you up, but it is better than being surprised to death. We are under attack. I'm accompanied by Lieutenant General Paul Malong, whom some of you might have heard about. He has not come here tonight because we are enjoying peace and stability. As you all know, he has been out there fighting for our peace to liberate our society. He is here to share military intelligence and his vast experience in military matters—and he can steer us in this attack to victory." Dombai hesitated for a moment and then he continued, "When there is an issue, it is men who have always addressed it. We now have a huge problem, comrades. We suspect that we have been invaded by the Arabs.

Chapter Four

They must be within our territory. We are the men in charge of this province. Countrymen, Arabs don't want the best for us. We have had peace for nearly a year, but it is officially over. Now is the time to brace yourselves for a serious fight. Let us show our enemies that we have not been sleeping during the peaceful times." There were murmurs, particularly from the enraged youth, baying for the blood of the raiders. Dombai concluded his speech with the signature declaration, "God bless you all, God bless South Sudan, and God bless our struggle."

Everyone clapped their hands in joy, some proclaiming "Asiele Oye! Asiele Oye!" and another part of the group crying, "AsielemOye! AsielemOye!" [*Some members could not pronounce the term SPLA; instead, they pronounced it as "Asiele" and SPLM as "Asielem." Some pronounced it as "Esfielem," because Dinkas and other tribes initiated their children by extracting the front upper teeth and they had difficulty pronouncing the letter P. Both SPLM (Sudan People's Liberation Movement) and SPLA (Sudan People's Liberation Army) had their humble origins in Gel Weng—SPLA would morph into the military wing and SPLM would be the political wing.*]

With the knowledge that General Malong was with them in their cause, they were excited and ready to confront the enemy.

Chapter Five

Riel and Nhier lay awake in their beds, restless. They had heard the jostling and shuffling outside their home. They got up and peeped through the spy hole on the wooden door and could see the men standing outside. The anxiety was palpable. *What could be wrong,* they wondered. Dombai opened the door with a fierce urgency that terrified the children. Riel and his sister rushed back to their beds.

"Riel!" Dombai called out, as he rushed into their room. "I'm leaving with the men waiting for me outside. I will come back. Until then, take care of your sister and your mother. You are now the man in charge." Dombai understood the risk of entrusting his young boy with the family, but sometimes, a man has to do what he has to do. He kissed Riel on the forehead and then kissed Nhier. "I love you so much, my daughter. Take care of yourself. Always respect your brother."

Dombai left the children's room and went to his wife, who was full awake by now, and peeping through the window, trying to make out what was going on outside. She looked shocked and worried. "Are the kids fine?" she asked with maternal apprehension.

"Yes, they are fine, dear. But I am leaving. It seems that we are under attack, and as men, we must take charge. I am lead-

Chapter Five

ing several young men to deal with the attackers. So you will have to forgive me as we go out and see if we can restore peace and order."

Abuk looked at him in the darkness and Dombai could feel her probing eyes. "As a leader, people expect a lot from me. I have to deliver. People expect me to lead this rebellion," Dombai continued, even as Abuk said nothing, as if silently protesting. "Gel Weng is now a large movement, and we should be safe and fine. You need not worry."

She started to say something but decided against it. Dombai concluded his speech with, "I love you, and please take care of my little ones." He kissed her and turned to leave. As he reached for the door, she managed to mutter in almost a whisper, "I love you. God be with you, my love," as tears rolled down her cheeks.

The soldiers were warming themselves, singing the "Asiele, Asielem" anthem. Dombai joined the other men and they trod northward. It was a path well worn by both raiders and traders. The men who were now preparing to fight were the same ones who conducted business between the north and south. Today they were fighters; in peaceful times, they were traders.

Abuk never stopped worrying about whether the men would return safely. The northern attackers were known for their sophisticated weaponry and ferocity—so savage that it defied comprehension.

PART II

Chapter Six

AS DOMBAI AND HIS MEN NEARED AWIEL, Dombai heard a blast and shouted, "RPG! [*Rocket-propelled grenade*] Comrades, down!" He hushed the men as he ordered them to crouch. Everyone lay down. A shot ripped through the warm, dry air.

The Southerners had decided to engage the government that had been marginalizing them. Secretly they had imported a cache of arms, and the men were impatient to use them. It took only a few minutes to plunge the whole community into chaos. Confusion reigned in Awiel, the state capital. People ran helter-skelter. Instantly, everyone in the town knew that this was not a "normal" raid. The AK 47, commonly used in wars in Africa, could not be heard above the blasts of the RPGs, tankers, and other sophisticated artillery. It dawned on the locals that the northerners had not stormed the town for the usual raid. They had come to take

Chapter Six

over and overthrow the local regime. The attackers had come to control the local authority, collect taxes, and impose their law over the Christian dominated area. Dombai and his troops were ill prepared to resist the well-organised and armed northern government troops.

Dombai and his men elected to fight, if only to repel the government side and give their families room to escape the brutality of the attackers. They were fighting to protect their freedom, their rights, their religion, and their territory. However, they were always considered rebels by the north Khartoum government.

That was the irony of it all. The raiders were seen as doing the right thing, despite their blatant looting and pilfering from the sweat of the innocent Southerners. The local administration, by resisting the attacks, had instantly been labeled as guerillas. Dombai and his troops decided to set up their base at the local administration office, calling it the Rebel Base Centre. Technically, the Southerners were homeless in their own country.

What Dombai could not predict was the impending displacement. The Khartoum government was hell-bent to possess their grazing lands and push them farther south. Because the Southerners were largely illiterate and most of them ignorant of the war mentality, they had not seen this coming. Later, they would learn that the government wanted the Arabs to move south and occupy the Abyei land that is originally occupied by the Dinka-Ngok. They also wanted to occupy Panthou that ancestrally belonged to the Dinka. Even Kiir-Adem land of the Malual-Dinka was highly coveted. Coincidentally, these parts are oil rich.

Chapter Seven

DOMBAI AND HIS GROUP WERE OUTGUNNED, of course, and could not hold the attackers; they reached Dombai's village almost effortlessly. His children Riel and Nhier escaped the brutality of the attackers only by the grace of God. When their mother went to their room, there was no sign of them. She was filled with worry and fear as she fled from the room, fearing the worst. She ran as fast as her feet could take her.

By the time Dombai and his men realised the futility of their efforts, the villages had been deserted. The people had escaped. The attackers took control of the area and within hours they had burned all the houses.

When Riel and his sister ran from their home, they had gone into the forests. They wandered through the thick foliage despite the presence of many venomous snakes and vicious wild animals. They prayed, muttering, "God guide us." After several days in the forests surviving on only fruits, they stumbled upon a village southeast of their village. They had come out of the forest unscathed.

Even here, the villagers lived one day at a time. Hide and seek from the attackers was the norm from their village to the north. Those who could not get away were shot, and their

Chapter Seven

dead bodies left to rot or to be a feast for hyenas and vultures. There was little time to mourn them. It seemed that the people had already shed a lifetime of tears. Death had become so normal to them that they just moved on. The wounded had to fend for themselves, as there was no means to move them. Tears were too precious to be wasted on a person soon to die, so the survivors saved them, should they themselves be shot. Individuals had become dehumanized to the point where death of another meant nothing, and each day that came was a gift. Death was ever-present—as near as the mouth to the nose.

All the more depressing was that the northerners would strike at will. Never before had the villagers known such misery. Riel and Nhier could not stay in the village for long, as it was soon under attack. They went back into the forest. Like many families in the forests, they survived on fruits. During the dry season they would eat dry fruits such as *atuek* and *pampamlaang* [*local, seasonal fruits*], and for their meat cravings, they caught birds and roasted them.

They often reminisced about better days when they lived as perhaps the happiest family in their village. The whereabouts of their caring father was unknown, but they hoped he was safe. Their mother was also missing. Riel relived the happy days when food and clothing were not an issue. The days ahead were uncertain, with death so near. Under such circumstances, providence was the only thing they could bank on—like on the day they were walking through the forest and spotted a hut that was in flames. Nhier, who was dying of thirst, saw a pot of water in the compound. She started to rush for it, but Riel restrained her. "It is not safe!" They hid in the nearby bush, waiting to see what would happen next.

Evidently the attackers had been there just a few minutes before they arrived. Nobody in their right mind would burn their own house. Although during times such as this, locals would employ various strategies to ward off the attackers. Riel was convinced that the attackers were hovering somewhere in the vicinity, so they remained hidden in the nearby bushes. As their eyes roamed wildly, someone came from behind the hut and started putting out the fire. He did so with tremendous trepidation, with all his senses on alert. Riel watched as the man tried to salvage what little he could, even as the dry, southward wind caused the fire to consume the hut more greedily. Assured by his actions and his dark skin that the man was a southerner, the two children were relieved and emerged from their hiding place.

They noticed that some people started trooping in from the forest. Back then, there was not much in terms of technology. No telephones. No Internet. While some countries in Africa at least had telegraphing, in the southern part of Sudan that was alien stuff—virtually unheard of. There was no way to tell people what was happening. Therefore, people would stay in the forest oblivious of the prevailing peace, however fleeting. Yet they had learned not only to survive, but to adapt to the climate and environment both in their homes and in forests. It was their second nature. Whenever there was a need or when tired of staying in the forest, they would send a few young men to survey the situation and determine if the Arabs had left. If the men came back, it meant there was peace, and the people could return to their villages. Sometimes the young men would take longer to return, but if they didn't return at all, it was assumed they had been killed; thus it was unsafe.

Chapter Seven

Riel and Nhier wanted to help the man whose house had burned, although at their age they could only do so much— but what they lacked in strength, they made up for with an overwhelming will to help, and their childlike sincerity went a long way. The man went on putting out the fire as the two children joined him. They did salvage a number of things. The man had been too consumed with containing the fire to recognize the children who were helping him. It was Riel who realized that the man was Tem, their father's business manager. They hugged him, all of them happy to see each other. Tem's family was still in the bushes. He had come back to see if the area was safe for his family to return, only to find his house ablaze.

"So, Riel, where is your father?" Tem asked as he patted his back.

"We really don't know. Since the day of the attack, we have never seen him," Riel said, looking down.

"Mmmm . . ." Then hoping for a positive answer, asked, "And your mother?"

Riel shook his head. "We haven't seen her either."

"I'm sorry," Tem said. "Now, you must wait for me here. I will go back and fetch the family from hiding. You will stay with us. You need not worry. This is like your family. Feel free."

But no sooner had Tem disappeared into the nearby bushes than a huge blast went off. The sound was louder than anything they had ever heard. The villagers had barely packed to get out of the bushes when they were on the run again. They were literally being smoked out. Riel and Nhier were again on their own, running for their lives. They missed home and the embrace of their parents. The stories their father told them before they slept. The food they ate. The shopping expeditions they used to go on with their parents. The sooner they could get back home with their parents, the better. They were too young to sustain themselves in the forest. If only they could connect with other villagers!

Death and war is no respecter of age. War affects everyone in equal measure, and death takes anyone it wants, whenever it wants. They wandered aimlessly in the forests, with Riel holding his sister's hand. They did not know if their mother was dead or alive. Neither did they know anything about their father. Days had become weeks, and weeks were slowly turning into months. During war and deprivation, people tend to lose a sense of time. Survival becomes the only instinct of importance.

One day when Riel sat under a fig tree, eating nothing but fruits and drinking water from a nearby pond, a wandering soldier stumbled upon him. It was a relief for Riel to see a human being, but more important, a southerner—and especially an adult.

"Young boy, what are you doing here?" the soldier asked Riel.

"We separated from our parents during the attack, so I'm on the run with my sister," Riel said, rather confidently.

"Where is your sister?' the man asked. Riel pointed toward the bush, where his sister had gone to relieve herself.

The soldier said, "Well, there is some camp nearby, to our East. I will take you there. Maybe you will be able to find your parents."

"Thanks. We will be grateful, uncle," Riel replied. [*It is common for African children to refer to adult males as "uncle."*]

Riel followed the man, with his sister in tow. Nhier was

Chapter Seven

now so tired and dehydrated that she could barely talk or walk. After several minutes of walking, they discovered they were not covering much ground. But their new "uncle" was a patient man, who understood the children's ordeal. From time to time, as the soldiers roamed in the forests, they found people who were too tired to walk dying and wasting away in the forests. Some would fall sick, or were just too hungry and dehydrated to lift their legs. Their strong will, battered by the sun, had long given up on the struggle. But the soldier had found something fascinating in children—they seemed to have a strong will in the face of the adversity.

Nhier was hungry and thirsty. Nobody was talking. They all looked tired. Even the soldier who had walked for many days on end looked equally fatigued. Even so, if they were to move any faster, he decided that he must carry Nhier on his back. Riel had to walk more briskly now and run from time to time, as he was lagging behind. They walked for many kilometres before finally nearing the camp. Never once did the soldier mention his name. He calmly put Nhier down, whispered to her in a conspiratorial tone that he was going to find out where their parents were and that he would come back with them, and walked away. The children believed him and continued to walk the remaining distance to the camp. The soldier, of course, did not come back. He had returned to the fighting.

PART III

Chapter Eight

FROM LIVING IN A TASTEFULLY FURNISHED HOUSE full of supplies and other luxuries, Riel and Nhier now lived under a tree. The home filled with the laughter, love, and peace they had always received from their parents was no more—possibly gone forever. Whatever the severity of the weather, without shelter, they had to endure it. The two children would cry the whole day when overwhelmed by hunger, exhaustion, and the long days and even longer nights. They had to invent a million ways of ducking and jumping the landmines. Danger was ever-present. When the northerners were not chasing them, they had to deal with wild animals seeking some human blood to quench their thirst.

Life was precious to them, but not to the government in Khartoum. The government wanted them dead. If they were to live, they had to convert to Islam. They loathed the forced Arabic education. They would never know peace as Christians or the Animists that they were.

Chapter Eight

Riel and Nhier, now counted among the thousands displaced from the Bahr el Ghazal region, had settled in a camp along the seasonal River Nile and were adamant that they would not change their religion. Other than the violence from the Khartoum government, forcing the Islamic religion on them was one of their biggest issues with the mostly Arabic, Muslim-dominated north. There was a widespread, shared belief that God created all human beings equal and each was entitled to their choice of how to worship Him.

The new camp was home to wives and children of the rebels fighting the Khartoum regime. Women now had to act as fathers and mothers. It was a terribly demanding job, especially because it involved keeping their children safe. Also in the camp were the elderly, who were too old to pick up arms and join the liberation war. Ironically, most of these people had fought against the British to liberate their motherland, only to see the country fall from the blatant discrimination and hatred perpetrated by Khartoum government.

Riel and Nhier were not the only children who had no parents, or whose whereabouts were unknown. A typical day for Riel and Nhier started with their leaving the camp to walk to the river for a bath, then come back to participate in the communal meal. The only food available was *abere*— dry kisira, which is a local food made from any cereal flour, mostly rice and millet. Abere is tasteless, so sometimes, if it was available, the communally appointed chef warmed some water, poured it on the dry kisira along with some cooking oil, salt, and sugar. It was magic! Prepared this way, the dish is called kisira. By the refugee camp's standards, that food was as good as Christmas.

As time went by, Riel and Nhier became more emaciated.

Riel thought of selling his coat in exchange for food in the camp, but then he became creative. Riel discovered fishing. Away from the prying eyes of their fellow refugees, he would go down to the river and catch some fish that they would later smoke. Sometimes, other refugees would join them in the fishing expeditions. Some of those lucky to access small wires would improvise them into fishing hooks, while others tried their luck with bare hands. Given the recent rains, the river overflowed with water that was teeming with several species of fish—all of them edible. Sometimes the fish washed up on the shore and when the water receded from the banks, the fish were left behind. They could be harvested without anyone breaking a sweat. When the rains went away and they could no longer find any fish, Riel sold his coat in exchange for abere. He was left with only a T-Shirt, his blue trousers and the boots that he had managed to sneak away from Warawar, in Bahr el Ghazal.

Now holed up in the Upper Nile region with people from different communities but equally affected, they were all Christians or Animists and were opposed to the north's forceful and brutal spread of Islam. The sheer brutality meted out by the Khartoum government on innocent people was unbelievable.

Chapter Nine

IN THE CAMP, DAYS DRAGGED BY SLOWLY and painfully. With nothing to do and so little activity, people spent their days swatting and swishing away the persistent flies that were a permanent fixture of their lives. Tsetse flies had a field day in making their lives miserable, with children suffering the most. One such day, Nhier saw her brother returning after a long day of hunting and fishing on stagnant swamps that had not yet dried off. Nhier had been hungry for the last few days that Riel had been away. She had been feeding on tree leaves and water. At times, salted water sufficed. So bad was the situation that even the fat girl in the next camp was getting thinner. As displaced people, they had no place to call home, yet anywhere was home as long as they were in the south.

To ward off the boredom of the day, Riel and Nhier sat outside the refugee camp minding the sun and watching those who were passing by, going about their business, unaffected by the war. They always thought about their father, and daydreamed about where he might be.

Dombai, their father, was now in Ethiopia, training with Mormor troops that had left Bahr el Ghazal as soon as the war broke out. He was their captain, leading a unit of the most revered soldiers. Often they would troop back into the country to

37

deal with troops from the north. Presently, they were holed somewhere between Eastern Equatorial and the Upper Nile region. Somehow, they had lost direction as they headed East toward Ethiopia. With no compass, Dombai had led his troops south without knowing whether they would pass safely.

Luckily the south was safe, save for the occasional confrontation from the Western Equatorial region and occasionally from Ugandans, aligned to the notorious warlord, Joseph Kony. They were determined, buoyed by the recent training of some of the soldiers in Cuba as well as the ammunitions they had been given. As they headed south, they stumbled upon Juba, the unacknowledged capital of the south, at that time controlled by the Khartoum government. They were ambushed by the government troops, causing them to head farther south as they scattered for safety. This only complicated and jeopardized their journey from Ethiopia more. Along the way, they were forced to change routes often. Sometimes, they had to raid some villages or smaller towns to acquire food and ammunitions. Again, they were lucky that more and more southern towns were joining the rebels, making their work easier.

As these unforeseen challenges weighed on Dombai's mind, the more removed he was from thoughts of his family. He was preoccupied by the deaths of his soldiers, who were dying at an unsustainable rate. Since they started the journey, his colleagues had died in tens, now inching toward hundreds of soldiers. Some died in the sudden ambushes and others could not keep up with the trek. In such a situation, if a man's spirit is broken, nothing could mend it. Yet he had seen many come to the brink of giving up, and a word of encouragement or even a bottle of water had helped add a day to their lives. The few times his family crossed his mind, he hoped that they would be fine; and in his most private thoughts, hoped that should he die, he would have died for a worthwhile cause—that he would be

Chapter Nine

remembered as a martyr, a freedom fighter, and that his family would get to enjoy the fruits of his struggle.

Little did he know that his children were presently fending for themselves, with Riel forced to step up to the task of feeding and protecting his younger sister. Little did he know that in the camp, life was incredibly difficult—for if he knew, perhaps he would have changed his mind and gone back to be with his children.

Nevertheless, he had to keep a proper frame of mind if he was to guide the soldiers whose spirits, understandably, were being crushed. Their mission was simple: Get to Ethiopia, receive training, obtain some ammunition, then come back and deal ruthlessly with the brutal Arabs who had razed their villages.

The people in the communities were constantly on the run. They had to forget about their worldly possessions. Their livestock and anything they owned had been left behind and was looted by the Arabs, who then sold it for close to nothing in the markets to the north. The Southerners were constantly alert, taking turns sleeping, allowing each other a chance to recharge for the trek to the southeast of the country.

As Riel and Nhier ate their meal, which could be their last, there was a huge blast, probably from an RPG. If it was not an RPG, then it had to be one of those artillery tankers. This sent cold shivers down their spines. Everyone in the camp looked across the river as a cloud of dust and smoke engulfed the other shore. Nhier held on to the plate of the unfinished food, ready to run. Everyone in the camp seemed to be jumping into the river and there was pandemonium—a swimming competition without any parameters—young and old, men and women, rich or poor. Riel had never seen so many people gripped with fear in his life. He instinctively grabbed Nhier's hand. They looked at each other, then ran toward the forest. Everyone was confused and didn't know where to run. Gunshots rent the air. Confounding everyone were the endless blasts that were getting nearer and nearer. Those who could not decide quickly enough, or were not agile enough, most certainly lost their lives that fateful day. Many more drowned. The people who could swim saved themselves, but those who could not, drowned.

Riel and his sister waded deeper into the forest. Nhier steadfastly held on to the plate, as it held their last bit of food until they could figure out how to survive. So far, providence and nature were on their side—they had survived the attack.

As they navigated their way through the forest, to their shock and horror they were slowed down by the number of dead bodies. Apparently these were people who had been shot and wounded, and died as they ran away. The brother and sister came face to face with a soldier hiding behind an anthill, shooting at the enemies. The soldier was one of the few men left behind in the camp to protect those who were fleeing. As was usual, the camp had been attacked by government troops. The soldier seemed to be a sharpshooter, because he took out many of the enemy. He was oblivious of the presence of Riel and Nhier. There were two other soldiers who were offering cover from behind, and they ordered them to get out of the line of fire. Bullets were flying by too close and falling behind them as they ran. The soldiers took cover behind a bush that surrounded the anthill. The two children were now caught in the crossfire. The other two soldiers were sharpshooters as well, and inspired confidence. Now all together, the three of them shot down the enemy soldiers with their machine guns. The children were overwhelmed by the power and sound of the gunshots. Nhier fell

Chapter Nine

down, and one of the soldiers had to carry her as they moved closer to the enemy. The one remaining enemy soldier was shot at close range.

Convinced they had done a perfect job, another soldier held Riel's hand and they made toward the forest. But his assumption that they had gunned down all the enemy soldiers was proved wrong when one of them shot at them. One of the soldiers discovered that his gun had no bullets. As he strived to load it again, the enemy relentlessly fired a number of shots their way. The bullets were coming fast, and fell at close range to the soldier who was able to shoot. He seemed unconcerned about his own safety. He had a certain iron determination that Riel admired, but Nhier was terrified.

For one fleeting moment there was silence as the five of them circled another anthill. But the soldier holding Riel's hand had been shot. He slowed down and as he fell, let go of Nhier's hand. He shouted at the two children to run down the hill and hide in a bush while the soldiers contemplated how to deal with the government troops that seemed inexhaustible. As the children ran off, the soldier who had been shot played dead for a few seconds, then adjusted his gun and pumped four bullets into an enemy soldier who was running toward them. When Riel was sure that the enemy soldier was dead, he ran uphill to attend to the wounded soldier. His leg was bleeding profusely. As the sun rose, Riel tore the soldier's trouser leg to give the blood room to flow. One of the other soldiers improvised a bandage out of some clothing, and wrapped it around his leg. He told his comrade he was lucky that the bullet had not hit a bone. It was a flesh wound, although a bad one. They had barely finished wrapping the bandage when it was blood-soaked. Nhier cried softly, with her head buried between her knees. One of the soldiers reloaded his gun, unsure if they had contained the government's soldiers, even if only temporarily. They also really wanted to teach the government a lesson.

What Riel did not know and will never know was that the soldiers had trained with American marines in the 1980s and had previously worked with the central government in Khartoum for a couple of years before they joined the rebel movement to liberate their people who were increasingly being repressed.

Now, as they cleared the site, no more gunshots could be heard. Certainly, the enemy had changed direction and opted to chase after the civilians—unarmed women and children.

As they ventured through the forest, they came across several bodies. There was no need to bury them because the vultures would descend on the bodies before the relatives could gather to give them a proper burial. Even so, the sheer number of those killed was overwhelming; those who were still alive could not risk staying behind to bury their dead. They had to run for their lives.

The soldiers asked Riel and Nhier to go into the forest toward the presumably safer side of the forest. The soldiers had to remain behind to ward off the northerners as well as any enemy troops. They also had to tend to their wounded comrade. The enemy was not as far away as they had imagined.

As the children wandered through the forest, Nhier still held the plate with the remaining portion of abere. They worked their way through the dead bodies. Although they were now used to seeing them, no one could know the kind of effect this had on their young and vulnerable minds. The

Chapter Nine

whole forest reeked of blood, smoke, and destruction. Riel walked along with his sister, not heading anywhere in particular, but with a remnant of hope that by some miracle, they would meet their parents. Through it all, God had guided them and provided for them since leaving Warawar—through the ambushes and the several hundred acres of forests they had covered south of Bahr el Ghazal. They had survived on very little food. They fed on wild fruits and they hardly cared if the fruits were poisonous. If anything looked remotely edible, they ate it. At times they had no people to interact with, and of course no place to call home. They hoped that they would not come across a Koor—a lion—since it was the most revered animal in the South Sudan jungles. Crickets filled the air with their noise, reminding the children of their existence. Birds chirped and flew freely in the sky, oblivious of the human suffering on the surface of the earth. But life no longer had meaning for Riel and Nhier. They walked deeper into the forest.

The three soldiers who had stayed behind managed to find reinforcements and they went after the enemy soldiers, shooting those who were wounded to ensure that they were dead with no chance of survival. This doubly outraged the Arabs. They responded with a full-fledged war; not with the conventional guns from previous African wars—the AK-47 or the RPG. No, they rolled to the south with tanks. The destruction happened unbelievably fast. They did not leave anything standing. Not a house. Not a wall. Not a tree. Even the brave American-trained soldiers and their leader, known as Chol, considered the risk and retreated as far back as necessary to be safe.

With no house, camp, or tree to hide behind, the surviving people were being pushed farther and farther south.

Chapter Ten

AFTER GETTING THROUGH THE FOREST, Riel and Nhier arrived at a new camp in the afternoon. Riel ran around the camp and begged for some food from those who had seen better days at the camp. He came back with water and abere. He was disappointed. The meal was hardly edible even for someone who had been starving and on the verge of death.

Nhier drank water and took some food. When she turned to look at her brother, his forlorn look was unsettling. She nudged him. "What is it, my brother? Are you okay?" Riel nodded his head, insisting that he was okay. "Come on, let us have this food together," she said as she held some on her hand, passing it to him.

Riel just looked at her. "I'm okay, just enjoy your food." After a while, Riel broke the silence. "There are no signs of our parents here. Our mother is not here. Our father also is not here. I gather that our father has gone to Ethiopia and he is now a general with Asielem [SPLM]. That is what the woman who offered me water and abere told me," Riel said as Nhier began to cry.

Riel wondered what he was going to do. *As we run for our lives, our parents have to fight, go to war, and risk everything so*

Chapter Ten

that we can live. If they fear, then the whole community will be wiped out.

Nhier was lost in her own thoughts. She mumbled a few words and made an attempt to ask questions, but what her brother had said about their parents was beyond comprehension.

They were exhausted and had nowhere to go, but they wanted to take a chance and find their way home. Maybe their mother was waiting for them there. Feeling helpless, they sat there with tears rolling down their cheeks. Riel had tried to restrain himself. If he cried, it would make Nhier cry even more. He was the source of courage that had sustained them in the forest and up to the camp. Although feeling disheartened, he still had hopes of a reunion with their family. The only news they had was that their father was alive, even though he was far way. But he was now an army general in the Asiele, Asielem movement, which was a big position in the SPLM movement. But they were more worried about their mother.

Riel and Nhier were like the soldier who is shot on the battlefield, but continues to fight while still wounded. Their spirits were wounded, but they soldiered on. Sometimes in the cold and sometimes without water or food, days turned into weeks; weeks turned into months; months turned into years. Life had proven very difficult for young Riel and his even younger sister.

Dombai and his men had no base; no place they could call their barrack—their headquarters, and where soldiers usually lived. They were always on the move so no one could trace where he and his men were or where they would sleep.

Riel, as his father had told him, was now a man on his own. He tried every day to be a better man, to encourage his sister and give her hope that God had good things for them, especially now that their father was a general in Asiele. "We will soon have a better life in the city, with plenty of food, bottled water, and new clothes. Life will be good. Dad and mum will be there to protect us and play with us. Mum will be cooking delicious food in the kitchen for us once again."

Nhier would smile and say, "When is this day coming? I am waiting for this day. I don't want to die. I will wait for this happy day. When that day comes, I will eat and eat and eat till I am full, so full that I will desire no more." She would close her eyes and pray, "Lord, grant me my wishes, bring us peace, and take us home."

Riel was determined, and believed that the war would end one day. And unless they died of hunger, thirst, or a bullet, they would surely live to reap the fruit of this struggle.

Their father, Dombai, had been shot three times in different wars and had survived them all. He was determined to bring peace to his people by all means necessary. He had led attacks and ambushes—he had been attacked and ambushed himself. But God had taken him through it all, and he believed that the dawn was near.

PART IV

Chapter Eleven

WHEN THE COMPREHENSIVE PEACE AGREEMENT was signed in 2005, Dombai was a brigadier in the army. He was heartbroken, homesick, and agonized every day, longing to see his family. He had not heard whether his wife and children were alive or not. It had been six years since Tem told him that he had seen the children at his village before an attack. But the village had long been deserted. No one lived there anymore. He heard that the market had been attracting enemies like moths are attracted to a lamp, so it was closed if only to lessen the attacks. There was no one left to ask the whereabouts of the villagers. Now with the ensuing peace, every soldier was asked to give names of their children and wife or wives in full, as the search party was about to be dispatched. Dombai repeatedly asked the soldiers, especially those who joined the movement much later, if they had ever come across his wife or kids or the names Abuk, Riel and Nhier. The answer was always no.

One day the news finally came—his children had been spotted in Panthou, miles away from Dombai's current barrack centre. Dombai immediately ordered some soldiers to go get his children and bring them to him. The person who had the information about Riel and Nhier had given the soldiers precise directions pinpointing the location, although he didn't know they were the children of a brigadier in Asiele. He had merely told a story of two remarkable children who had waded through the jungle and forests, inexplicably surviving all the attacks waged by the north.

When the soldiers located them, they bought them new clothes for the trip, food, and clean water. Riel and Nhier were so happy, and could not stop smiling at each other. They were eager to see their father, and hoped that he had not changed too much. They were equally eager to see their mother, Abuk.

By dawn the following day, Riel and Nhier were reunited with their father who now had a thick moustache, was slightly overweight, and somewhat changed, but he was excited to see his children. Riel was taller and older, but lankier, and Nhier was thin to the point of emaciation.

In a voice filled with trepidation, Nhier asked, "Where is mum?"

Dombai wondered what he would tell his daughter, who was already shedding tears over the emotional reunion. Then the three of them were crying. No words or explanations were necessary. The kids knew that their mum was not with their dad, nor had she been.

He hugged them tightly, squeezing them to his chest. "I haven't seen her since 1993. I thought you were with your mother!" Dombai could only imagine the suffering his chil-

Chapter Eleven

dren had undergone while he was busy in the bush, liberating his kinsmen.

"You will be fine with me. I will take good care of you, and buy you food and clothes. You will have shelter and you will go to school too. Let us hope your mother is fine, wherever she is. Do not worry much now my children, you will be with me forever—nothing will separate us again," he assured them.

It wasn't long after the family was reunited that a radio call came for Dombai. The brigadier was needed on the line, as he was the commander in charge of the barrack. The call of duty came from Dr. John Garang.

"Hello comrade, you have a duty to attend to in Kiir Adem. Please comrade, go and survey the border and do demarcation with our army. We will sign the peace agreement tomorrow and we want our forces to advance to the north, so that when we have the ceasefire we will have secured our borders."

"Okay comrade, I will do as you say. I salute you. Goodbye." The joy of being with his children had been severed before it could be savoured. The order from the boss had cut the reunion short.

The radio call came at 6 o'clock that morning, and by 8 o'clock that same morning, he and his army had started the journey up the Kiir River to secure the border.

Riel and his sister were left again, but it was better that they were home. At least this time they had hope that their father would come back very soon after the mission. What encouraged them was the signing of the peace agreement. There was going to be no more war, no more Arab brutality, no more running, no more hiding, and no more confusion.

A few kilometres from Kiir River, Dombai and his army were ambushed by soldiers from the north. Dombai was shot in the chest, his left leg was torn to shreds, and he lost a lot of blood. His bodyguards carried him away from the battle in search of a safe place. Dombai's men scattered, but Tem, who was Dombai's deputy, took charge and their army rallied. After six hours of fierce fighting they managed to chase the enemy away. The northern soldiers were defeated, although they had left many of Dombai's men wounded. The few from the north who escaped from that battle never thought of going to war with Asiele again; they understood how skillful and trained the army of the south had become.

Dombai's men killed the wounded enemies while taking their own wounded infantrymen to a helicopter that airlifted them and their leader, Dombai, to the hospital. The problem was that the Juba Hospital was congested and had very few - doctors.

The comprehensive peace agreement was signed, and there was a big celebration in Nairobi.

Riel and Nhier were watching the celebration on television when a man came into the room and said, "Your dad is in the hospital. He was shot this afternoon."

Crying, they reached for each other and held hands as they screamed from their pain. They did not know what would happen now. They were rushed to the hospital to see him, but by the time they arrived, their father had been taken to a Nairobi hospital. Even before they could beg for a ticket to Nairobi from a Good Samaritan, Dombai was on his way to the United States. His condition was critical. The government of South Sudan was taking care of his treatment. That evening a new brigadier was brought in to head the division.

Chapter Eleven

Riel and his sister were kicked out of their house and found themselves in the streets; not in the bushes, streams, and valleys of the war, but in the streets with the careless drivers of Asiele. Their tears had washed away all of their short-lived joy. Everything their father had promised them was now a dream—just a flicker of their imagination.

In the hot weather of Juba, Riel had to provide for his sister, as a big brother should do. In the days after their father was shot, they joined several other children in the streets. It was overwhelming—their mother's whereabouts were unknown and their father's condition was critical; his survival hung on a thread.

Chapter Twelve

The only thing Riel knew about his father was that he had been taken to California State Hospital. He had no idea where California was, except that it was in the United States, a place far away from Sudan. He could not be sure that was even true. Perhaps the South Sudanese government had killed their father in the hospital. Riel knew that those the government hated *disappeared* from the hospitals or were killed in their beds and were reported to have died because of their health condition.

But Riel could not imagine that happening in the United States. After all, the U.S. was an open and just society, as he had learnt from the rumour mills. Nobody hated his father; he was a good friend to Dr. Garang. He had never rebelled against Asiele, neither had he ever stepped on anyone's toes. They believed their father was a good man, climbing up the Asiele ranks to be a brigadier meant he must have been one of the most respected officers.

At Jebel Market in Juba, Riel and Nhier got themselves a *rakuba*—a shelter with a roof made of patched, rusty sheets of iron filled in with grass at some points. There was no door. *Sherkania*, a mat made of grass, was applied to the walls. A full-grown man would not be able to sleep in it. The bed was

Chapter Twelve

an old mattress they found at the barrack, once used by the Arab soldiers long before the Comprehensive Peace Agreement. It was land with no title deed, but who has a title deed in Juba anyway? However, because they were young, an Asiele soldier could come at any time and kick them out or threaten to shoot them. That was life in their new city of Juba. Only guns and muscles counted for anything. Pistols and force were the tactics used to get anything done in political and economic struggles. They had to adapt.

Chapter Thirteen

"MORNING, NHIER, WAKE UP! It is another good morning. Have some water." It was barely 8 o'clock, but the scorching sun was already burning through Juba's atmosphere, and water was the first thing you took before you could figure out the day.

Nhier opened her eyes. The light was too bright. The sun was too strong to motivate her to start her day. She opened her eyes and closed them again, and then she opened them, slightly. "Morning, Riel. It's really hot today."

"Yes, it has always been hot in Juba," Riel replied and then asked her, "Are you okay now that you find the weather so different here?"

"Yes, I am fine my brother, it is just that I am sweating so much, which is not normal for me."

"You will be fine. God has a way, always," Riel said as he closed his eyes to say a prayer. He had come to believe that one had to close their eyes to pray.

The mattress was soaked with sweat, so Riel took it outside to let the hot sun dry it and disinfect it a bit. Nhier was left sitting in the rakuba with her knees touching her chin. There was no breakfast, but she was far more worried about lunch and water. Drinkable water was sold in Juba, if one had money to buy it.

Chapter Thirteen

Outside where Riel took the mattress were some Asiele soldiers. They were walking, guns strapped to their backs, chatting and smiling. At a distance were Asiele military tankers covered from the view of the public and from the dust. A few meters from their rakuba was the house of a military captain, and right in front of their rakuba was another, larger rakuba. Riel could not tell how many lived in that one. Sometimes there were more than ten people who chatted late into the night. In the morning, they would come out one after the other. Riel wondered if they had slept on top of one another. The most shocking of all was that there were two women in that particular rakuba. Riel failed to understand how they all slept in a 10 by 5 meter rakuba. But that was not his problem—he had other things to worry about, like food and water, and the hot sun of Juba that forced people to take water every thirty minutes.

When Riel would go to the Ministries of the President's Office, seeking help and support for them as orphans, Nhier remained behind and spent her days in that small rakuba of two square meters. They wished to go to school, have a better shelter and better food; not live by luck and the grace of a Good Samaritan. The security was not good where they lived. There were times when the Asiele soldiers got drunk and would shoot at each other as they quarreled, but in most cases they would shoot up in the air in celebration of the month-old independence since the signing of the Comprehensive Peace Agreement. The solders also celebrated ceasefire whenever they were drunk.

Riel spent his days at the gate trying to see the Minister of Education or the Minister of Youth, and wished that there were a ministry of planning for children because he would have tried to visit that as well. The way he was dressed prevented him from getting any closer than the gate. In torn clothes, dirty and dripping with sweat, he was part of the growing population of street urchins. He would not be allowed anywhere within ten feet of government offices. He looked like a stray rabid dog that needed to be kept at bay for the safety of the people. He bathed in the mornings, but as soon as he stepped out of the house, he began to sweat. He sometimes got to the gate earlier than 6 o'clock, but still he could not get in. No matter how hard Riel tried to be friendly in approaching the military soldier at the gate, he would always chase him away.

The Ministry of Gender seemed to be specifically targeting women. Riel often saw women gathered at the gate, milling around and quarrelling. With little knowledge of English, Riel thought that gender meant ladies and women—specifically widowed or divorced women. He understood that he would definitely not be allowed in since he belonged to neither group. Traditionally, men were the ones who went out to look for food for their families, so when a woman went out for this purpose, it meant that she must be a widow or a divorced woman. Therefore, Riel believed that those women were either divorcees or widows who had lost their husbands during the war. It was partly true, considering the number of casualties caused by the war. Also, some of the dead men could have been polygamists leaving behind many widows.

As a child of a freedom fighter, he could only hope that his father would not be among those sacrificed for the freedom. He felt that he deserved a better life—both as a son of a great fighter and as a South Sudanese survivor of the war. But who would care about other people's survival in a society that

Chapter Thirteen

was quickly becoming man-eat-man? It was as though they had never been through a war. Nobody cared about others, especially when they had power. That power was corrupting their minds.

Riel spent his days under a tree with a few others who could not manage to see the minister. They would chat and laugh as if all were well, but Riel would be thinking about his sister, and how he always had to leave her at their rakuba with no food or water. He knew that Nhier hoped he would be able to bring her something to eat at the end of the day, but he was out there doing nothing except praying in his heart. The sun was too hot for him to walk around looking for any manual work to do. As the conversation went on under the tree, Riel was not listening to their chatter; he had a big problem and a debate was going on in his own mind of survival versus death. Although he and Nhier could now rest more peacefully, life was still very hard in their new jungle.

It was fast approaching 2 o'clock, and there was not yet any hope of seeing one of the minsters. People were streaming back to their offices after lunch. Some would come in their cars, drive past the tree, and go to the parking lot. Others would come walking on foot; they were the ones who went across the road to mama Zara's or mama Arek's restaurant to grab some bread and beef. None of the working class cared about the young boys who were always sitting in the hot sun, waiting to see the boss—and maybe for something to eat.

"Hey, young man!" A guy who just came from lunch and had forgotten to buy himself bottled water called on Riel to go and bring water for everyone under the tree. This was a normal thing for a South Sudanese native to do whenever he was with his brothers, but Riel thought he was daydreaming. Then someone patted his shoulder, gave him twenty-five South Sudanese pounds, and asked him to go buy seven bottles of mineral water.

"Were you sleeping, young boy?"

"No sir, I was not sleeping," Riel replied in a soft voice. He then took the money and rushed across the road. In a short while he was back, carrying the bottled water in a paper bag. Riel received ten pounds as appreciation from the guy who sent him. He was so happy to get the money, even though he didn't show any emotion apart from saying, "Thank you." Then to be polite, he smiled at the man.

Life had taught him that there was nothing to smile about. Riel had no plans or programs for any particular day; he lived one day at a time, and depended on chance. Whatever a particular day had to offer, be it good or bad, he had to take it— he had no choice. That day, with the ten pounds the man had given him, he bought *fuol* and *hesh* (beans and bread), which were commonly found in nearly every restaurant in Juba, and bottled water. It cost him five pounds—an arm and a leg as far as he was concerned. He kept the rest of the money for dinner the next day.

When he arrived at home, he found his sister sobbing. She was hungry and she needed some food. "Please cheer up; I have come with some food." Nhier sat up, wiped her eyes with her left hand, and got ready to eat. They ate and drank water, and soon Nhier was smiling and talking.

"How was your day my brother? I missed you so much when you were away. I actually washed your clothes." She pointed at the folded clothes in the corner—two torn hand-me-down-trousers and a T-shirt that had seen better days.

Chapter Thirteen

If they ate lunch, Nhier was sure there would be nothing to eat until the next lunch. But there were times when Riel would come home with nothing. On those days, they would walk to the Nile to drink water and then come back to their rakuba and sleep. Even so, Nhier had gained weight since they emerged from the forest where they hardly ate anything. However, life in the bush was preferable to their life now, after independence. They had to beg to survive. The best places to beg on weekends were the Da Vinci along the Nile and Jebel lodge down the mountain. Weekdays in the city there was a fair chance that a Good Samaritan would offer them money or food, but on weekends that was rare. People were busy with their social lives. Riel and Nhier lived one day at a time.

Chapter Fourteen

"IF ONLY I COULD MEET WITH THE MINISTER of Education, our lives would change. He would take us to school I am sure," Riel said to Nhier, smiling almost wistfully.

"Our lives will change? How? Where would the minister take us?" Nhier wondered how Riel could find anyone in Juba who would offer to help them. Juba was infested with greedy politicians who swarmed the city like hungry locusts. Only her father was brave enough to sacrifice anything for their country.

"He will take us to school and provide us with better housing and food," Riel replied.

Excited about this possibility, Nhier jumped up from the floor where she had been sitting. "Meet him, please, and take me along with you. Do you think they will allow me to see him? Oh, I hope so!" When will this happen?"

"I can't take you with me. I am not sure when I will meet him. It is not easy to see him. The guards at the gate are very rude. They have never allowed me into the compound."

Nhier was disappointed and said, "Too bad for us. What are we going to do now?"

"I will keep on trying; maybe I will try to see the president, though this is the hardest of all."

Chapter Fourteen

Nhier laughed sarcastically. "Tell me you are joking. If you cannot see the minister, how will you see the person who appointed him? Seriously, Riel? The president of the Republic of South Sudan? You haven't said anything funny today so let me take it as a Sunday joke." Nhier turned her face away from Riel. The hope she had felt just moments ago was gone. She could not see any way out of their miserable life.

Riel washed his hands and started patting his legs to remove the dust. The sun was hot. Only crickets would dare to question the sun by making noise at that time of the day. There was minimal traffic in Juba on this day. Only land cruisers, hardtops, jeeps, and cars that had air conditioners were on the road. Riel and Nhier could see the main road from their rakuba. No one in his right senses would dare walk during the afternoon sun. Many sat sheltered under unfinished, two-story buildings, sipping tea, smoking shisha, and having a good time, enjoying the rare cool but dry wind that swept through the building.

Cars with tinted windows went by. These were owned by those who claimed to be strugglers of the civil war, and now had an independent country. Some of those individuals acted as if they had been on the front lines during the civil war, and yet chances are they were not. Most of their stories of the liberation war had come from something they heard or read in the newspapers. Riel heard great names such as Salva Kiir, Dr. Riek Machar, Paul Malong, and Kuol Manyang at social gatherings, while others claimed that they knew them personally. Some even said they fought together with them on the front lines of the battlefields. Those claims were unverifiable, of course, but Riel didn't bother to be captivated by those tales, as he seriously doubted that they were true.

Nhier had yet to venture out of the rakuba to see what life in Juba entailed. If she had gone out, she would have encountered men gathered under a tree beside the road or under buildings where some woman would sit serving tea, jebna, chai leben, and chai sada—all ordered simultaneously by the constantly impatient customers. Instead, she chose to stay at home, longing for Riel to come back and tell her the day's stories.

Riel tried daily to see the Minister of Education or the Minister of Youth and Culture, but all his efforts were in vain. He finally lost hope and thought of other ways to live his life.

Chapter Fifteen

INTRIGUE WAS PART OF JUBA'S POLITICAL LANDSCAPE. One evening word went around that the president was to dissolve the cabinet. Information had been leaked from someone in the office of the president's staff to one of the daily newspapers. No one was totally convinced that this was true. Only time would tell. The president dissolved the cabinet three days later, and the public was unsure as to who was going to be appointed to fill the vacant positions. There was an air of uncertainty that hovered over all of Juba.

Riel had heard all about this. Young as he was, he had no voice over the government's decisions, but he hoped that whoever who was going to be appointed would be friendly and approachable—especially the Ministry of Education. He and his sister could certainly use some help getting into a school.

For the couple of weeks that the president was still consulting with his advisors over a new cabinet, there was no point in Riel going to the ministries. He had to change directions and try his luck elsewhere. The first two days he went to Thongpiny, an advanced residential area north of Juba, but there was nothing there; only some rich guys seated in well spruced streets, under trees, and the better hotels that were in that part of the city. Riel could not gain access to the crowd, so he changed his direction on the third day and went to Juba market to look for a job.

There were many social gatherings there, and it gave Riel a flicker of hope. However, he discovered that some boys of his age were also there trying their luck. Most of them were cleaning cars. Riel asked a young man who was cleaning one of the cars, "Is that your father's car?" Of course he knew from the way he was dressed that it could not be his father's car.

"No, I own the carwash. Juba Town is divided and we wash cars for a fee. Five pounds per car. Are you new here?'

Riel answered, "Yes and no. I have been around, but not in Juba Town." And then hesitatingly he asked, "So . . . can I . . . work with you?"

"Sure, you can join me. My colleague left three days ago for his state and he has not yet come back. The people of Mading Awiel have some festivities that my friend has gone to attend. They are the civilized Dinka of the Dinka community," he added.

Riel smiled, and immediately without preamble or any training, he took a bucket of water and started working. The boy showed him the territory lines and told him that whenever they crossed the lines, there would be a fight. Toward the south were some older boys in their mid-twenties. Some were school dropouts, due to lack of school fees. They could not find any job and now they worked there. They were the ones who came up with the system of dividing and demarcating parking space in various territories, and designated where the cars would be washed.

After Riel and the boy whom he came to know as Tony

Chapter Fifteen

finished washing the car, the owner came to pick it up. He was talking on his phone and held the keys in his other hand. Then another phone rang in his trouser pocket. He seemed to be in a hurry as he reached for the other phone in his pocket, and also managed to press the automatic car lock and opened the car door. He got into the Land Cruiser, closed the door, and sat there for a while talking on his phone while Riel and Tony stood in the hot sun, waiting to be paid. The car windows were not tinted so Riel could see the man. When he finished his conversation on the phone, he made another call, and then hung up. He waved at them, and then drove away without paying Tony and Riel for their efforts.

Riel asked Tony why he didn't pay. Tony said, "That is normal, my friend. At least he did wave at us as a sign of appreciation." As Riel discovered, the customers not paying, even though they were the ones who authorized the boys to wash their cars, was quite normal. They would say that they did not have change or they did not have money that day. Others just ignored them and drove away. Riel learned that in that business, they lived by luck and chance. Their survival was determined by those who had enough—and their commitment to honour their part of the transaction. If their customer was honourable, well, and good, Riel and his friend survived for another day. Riel knew that he had gotten a new job.

Riel and Tony walked back toward the shade. The wind was blowing, but it was hot. The area was congested with people. Some sold water from an icebox filled with ice stones. Riel squeezed himself into a small bit of shade under the extension of a building, and beckoned Tony to join him. Riel was sweating as he waited for Tony to buy some water. When he finally managed to buy some, he brought Riel a bottle of mineral water, which was about half-frozen. That was not a problem considering the high temperatures that would make it warm soon. The cold water could not stop the sweating. For a while his body contained the sweating, but then the heat surged and he started to sweat again. Riel took another sip, then tried to read the writing on the bottle. He finally gave up. He didn't know how to read very well, although he had tried to learn some elementary transactional Arabic.

It worried Riel when Tony told him how the big boys who washed cars on the northern side of the line harassed him at times. They were never happy with his presence, especially because he was younger than they were. They considered him unnecessary competition and told him that they would beat him up if they felt like it.

"I have never seen them smile," Tony said, as a car pulled up that was almost identical to the car that left without paying. Tony rushed over to the driver and inquired, "Can I wash your car, please?"

The driver asked how much he would charge to wash the outside. The rest of the passengers in the Land Cruiser Hardtop had gotten out of the car and rushed to the shade.

Tony said, "Only five pounds."

"Okay, please hurry up. I won't be long here." Riel was standing by with a rag and buckets of water as the negotiations took place, waiting for the go-ahead from Tony to start washing the car.

Riel stood on one side of the car and Tony on the other, both of them washing it as fast as they could. Riel could not think about the scorching sun and the sweating. They hurriedly cleaned the car and by the time the driver came back, it

Chapter Fifteen

was all clean. They pocketed their shared five pounds and went back to chat in the shade.

Life for Riel was getting better every day. At least most days he would go home with twenty pounds; and if it was a bad day, going home with seven or eight pounds was better than going home empty-handed like things used to be.

The thugs (the older, bigger boys) had not been so bad, until one day when Riel saw a car come and park at their parking space when they were not there. The car was very muddy. It might have come from Barr Road, which was the muddiest road known in the Equatorial State. The driver got out of the car and looked around. Since no one was around, he walked a few meters and saw Riel seated with a bucket next to him. He beckoned him over and Riel ran toward him. "Yes Sir!" he said.

"Can you wash my car over there? I will pay twenty-five pounds. I know it's very muddy."

"Sure, I will," Riel said as he looked around to see if the big boys were around. He wondered where they were. Tony had gone away and nobody knew where. Riel was in a dilemma. He looked around again to see if the bigger boys were hiding, then took his bucket and washing powder over to the car and started cleaning it. When he was almost finished, he again looked around to see if the big boys would find him in their territory, and there they were—three of them, sitting in the shade.

"Mmmm . . . we are lucky guys—we have found him today!" the first boy said, as though they had been waiting for the day when he would get into their trap.

Riel was frightened. "It's not me! I am new here!"

The oldest one of the crew drew his lip up in a sneer and

said, "We know, and we have been looking forward to this. We run this street." The three of them continued to sit in the shade and watched Riel walk toward them.

"Okay, can you please take over and wash? I was helping since you were not around," Riel said.

"No, you have to finish it and bring us all the money," The first boy said.

Riel could see on the third boy's face that he was quite sympathetic with him, but didn't have the guts to say anything. The other boys didn't seem to be his type. Life must have forced him into such company for survival.

Riel finished washing the car, and as soon as he was paid, the thugs took the money. It was like vultures tearing up a hapless young antelope that had been run over by a speeding a car. They roughed him up, turned his pockets inside out, and took everything, even the other money he had earned that day in his own territory.

Riel went back to his territory's shade with swollen eyes, holding back the tears. When Tony came and found Riel in that condition, he knew instantly what had transpired, but chose to inquire from Riel to be sure.

"Are you fine?" Tony asked as he sat down next to him.

"I am fine, Tony, but the big boys took all my money."

Tony was furious. "What?! Why? Why would they do that?" Tony got up from his stone where he had been sitting and started to walk toward the big boys' territory.

When Riel realised where he was going, he caught up with him and grabbed his arm. "Wait! Listen first!" He told him what had happened about his washing the car in their territory, but Tony didn't want to listen and he removed his arm from Riel's grasp.

Chapter Fifteen

In a matter of seconds, Tony was confronting them. "Hey, return Riel's money!"

They smiled arrogantly at Tony as they nodded their heads and retorted, "So, you have come to fight. What if we do not return it? What will you do?"

Tony was a man of action, and with his anger swelling out of control he was ready to beat them up. He said, "Return Riel's money and take only what belongs to you!" Then he went straight to the first boy's pocket and tried to remove the money. In a split second, a hard slap landed on his face. Tony fell down and Riel rushed to help him, but then the first boy kicked Riel from behind and he fell on top of Tony. The second boy gave both of them slaps and then the whole bunch fell on them punching, kicking and beating them severely. The third boy realised that it was getting out of hand and tried to stop them from beating the younger boys any further. Had it not been for the crowd that had gathered around and threatened to beat the entire mob, they probably would not have stopped. The three of them got away, Tony and Riel had been thoroughly beaten, and Riel's money had not been returned.

Riel and Tony came to when the sun was nearly setting. They decided to work no more, or at least for a while, and said good-bye to each other as they parted ways.

Riel had to walk home slowly because of the injuries he had suffered from the beating. From Uobo town to Jebel Market was about six kilometres.

Nhier was worried—it was unusual for her brother to be so late. They had never before lit a fire in their rakuba. That night Nhier went to the soldiers' barrack to borrow fire. She made a fire from pieces of wood she had gathered so there would be light, since it was so late and dark.

When Riel finally made it home, he was very tired, hungry, and aching from the beating. Nhier welcomed him home. He was not carrying any paper bag, so Nhier knew it was another bad day in the "office," and they were going to sleep on an empty stomach.

"Welcome home brother, how was your day?"

"All is fine, Nhier, just that I got beaten up today," Riel said.

"Who beat you?" Nhier asked.

"Some big boys in Juba Town, but all is okay. I am much better now. I am only worried about my friend Tony. I do not know how he is feeling now."

"Who is Tony?" Nhier asked.

"A new friend I work with in Juba Town. We work together at washing cars."

"Okay, I wish him well, he will be fine." Nhier did not even ask about food; she understood the situation. The good thing about Nhier was that she made sure there was enough clean Nile water in the house. Riel took a bath and after finishing, he stood out in the dark night to dry for he had no towel to dry himself. After his body was dry he put on his clothes and entered their tiny rakuba. He talked to his sister for a few minutes, but when she soon fell asleep, Riel began to think about the past. He particularly remembered days when it rained while they were in the forest. Soon, he drifted off to sleep.

The president had mostly forgotten the freedom fighters, but some had been appointed to his new cabinet. However, the president had no time for the children of the freedom fighters, or support for them—even in terms of education.

Chapter Sixteen

AFTER THE NEW CABINET WAS ANNOUNCED, Riel was back at the ministry's gates again. He hoped that the ministry would at least help his sister. For him, it was all but over in matters of schooling. If there was no education for a boy, at least a boy could be a criminal; if he does get an education but does not get a job, he could still be a criminal. What worried him most was that a girl's options were limited, dismal, and even at times horrifying. It was either marriage to some old man or prostitution. Worse, it was forced labour or human trafficking.

Within a week of trying to see the minister, Riel was finally allowed to see him. After being introduced, he was tense and did not know how to express himself. Nhier was with him that day. She broke the silence, "Sir, we are children who lost our parents and now we are struggling to survive every day. We're the children of Brigadier Dombai."

Riel found his courage and said, "Yes sir, we would like to get educational support, food, and shelter because at the moment we stay in a small rakuba near the barrack, and we're really struggling."

The minister hesitated for a moment and then said, "Yes, my children, I knew your father very well. He was a courageous man. I hope you will grow up to be like him, Riel." He paused and then continued, "Okay—for the education, food, and shelter, the ministry is not able to support individuals, but we have a program underway." He reached for his wallet, removed a bundle of money, and as he counted it out said, "Take these five hundred pounds in the meantime, and I will be sure to find something for you. I can have your sister come and stay with me."

Nhier exclaimed, "Yes, I want to do that, but I cannot leave my brother!"

"You can go Nhier, I will be fine," Riel said, even as he was feeling sorry for himself. He wondered why everyone was so unfair to boys. They wanted to make girls happy, but cared less about boys.

Nhier refused the minister's offer to stay with him, so he slipped the money back into his wallet and led them to the door. "Okay, go and we'll be in touch again and talk it over. I'll see you next time."

Riel and Nhier walked out, both of them disappointed. Although they had finally been able to meet with a minister, they knew they would never see him again. They went home holding hands and chatting, just trying to comfort each other. On their way, they bought food and mineral water. They went home and spent the rest of their day in their rakuba.

Riel never went to the ministry again, nor did he even think about it. He had to try a new life, a new hustle, and search for another job.

"This life has to come to an end, my sister. Now I will have to do whatever it takes to survive. No job is a dirty job. We need to have food, water, and shelter. We still cannot even afford the basics. But we will get them, I assure you," Riel said as he stared at the bamboo wall.

Chapter Sixteen

Nhier sat and put her arms on his brother's shoulders as she listened intently. "Yes, we are still struggling, but we should be used to this life. Seven years of struggle in the bush and the bullets we have escaped was nothing compared to the brutality from the government. I will help you; I will go to work so that we can save for the school fees for next year."

"No, I won't allow you. You are still young, my sister. You should be cooking for us." They both laughed at Riel's stern voice.

Nhier asked, "That is how young you think I am?"

"No, it's how much I care for you," Riel replied.

"Okay, but what is there to be cooked? There are no *sufurias* [cooking pans] and plates; actually there is nothing to cook!"

Riel smiled and said, "Soon there will be too much. Do you believe in God?"

"Yes, of course I do. What do you think?"

Riel assured her, "No! It is not what I think. I only wanted to know if your idleness would have changed your mind."

"I believe in God. I will never forget Him. He is the only one I can trust and I turn to when people like the minister betray us and the sacrifice my father made for this nation. Apart from you, my brother, God is my only provider." Riel nodded his head in agreement.

They were silent, each of them imagining what life would be like in the days to come. Darkness was approaching fast and Riel as the food provider had to figure out his plans for the next day. He thought of something he wanted to say to Nhier, but she had fallen asleep with her head on his shoulder. He laid her down slowly, so as not to wake her up. Then he lay beside her, looking at the ceiling. His face was gloomy and stress was building up. He worried about where he would find a job or food and clean water the following day. He stayed awake until midnight, thinking and trying to make plans for the following day. Nothing was coming to him. The silent night passed with no disturbance; it was not like most days when they would hear shootings and screams. It was a rare peaceful night indeed.

Early the next morning Riel woke up, washed his face, and set off to Juba Town in search of an opportunity. Nhier was still sleep when Riel left, so he closed the door behind him.

After he had been walking for a while, he was passing by some shops, lost in his thoughts, when he came across a fifty-pound note in the street. He picked it up, hardly able to believe his good luck. He smiled and tucked it in his pocket while looking around to see if anyone had seen him. When he crossed the road, there were some boys looking at him. These were orphans who lived on the street. They had seen Riel pick up something. Riel had eye contact with the most notorious of the boys, and the rest of them started racing toward him. He bolted. As he was running, he took a sharp corner, hoping he had lost them, but he was met with a furious punch from one of the street boys that knocked him to the ground.

"Where is the money?" the boy demanded.

"I don't have any money," Riel said as he reached to his pocket and removed papers.

"You must be kidding me," the bully thundered. "Who do you think we are? We run these streets. What is your name?" He then reached into Riel's pocket and removed a note of fifty South Sudanese pounds. The rest of the boys surrounded him as he lay on the ground, vulnerable. "Apart from being a liar, you are also a thief. Where did you get this money?"

Chapter Sixteen

"Mmmm . . . I . . . I . . ."

The bully got angrier and kicked him. "Where did you get the money?" he bellowed.

Riel couldn't get any words to come out of his mouth. He was terrified. The bully hit him some more, and then the rest of the boys descended on him, kicking, slapping, and dragging him on the ground.

After he was beaten, Riel was taken to a corner where the streets boys had their "office." He was interrogated, and then given an assignment; he was to report in daily and bring them money—ten pounds. Riel wondered how on earth he was going to get ten pounds to give to these thugs when he couldn't even earn five pounds for dinner for himself and his sister. Somehow he would have to find a way.

He was now part of the city's gang, and he was going to learn from the very best. He had only one thing motivating him, and that was Nhier's schooling. All he wanted was for his sister to go to school. He could not bear the thought of her being on the streets. To that end, he told himself, he would endure anything. He just had to figure out how to deal with the street bullies whose only claim to fame was that they had been on the streets longer. But he knew one important thing: bullies of all ages and sizes are generally cowards.

BOOK TWO

The Theatre of Hope

Introduction

"THE HIGHEST RESULT OF EDUCATION IS TOLERANCE," observed the blind and deaf American author, Helen Keller. Where people are educated and literacy levels are relatively high, there tends to be tolerance to new ideas, perspectives, and opinions. Such ideas or opinions may not be necessarily consistent with our ideals, but we learn to tolerate such differences for there is power in diversity.

Optimists who thought that Africa would be liberated after Independence (more than five decades ago for most of the countries) were in for a rude shock and disappointment. Many countries degenerated into wars. Consequently, they have lagged behind economically and in all developmental aspects. Suffice it to say, many of these countries are immensely endowed with minerals and natural resources that only require equitable distribution for Africa to ben on par with the rest of the world.

Such countries include Democratic Republic of Congo, Liberia, Angola, Sierra Leone, Guinea-Conakry, Benin, Somali, Ethiopia, Sudan, and Eritrea. All of these countries have been a source of instability to neighbouring countries that have had to provide refuge for the war escapees as well as provide the basic needs for the refugees throughout the war

Book Two: Introduction

periods. These countries are not usually in a position to feed their own population, let alone the refugees.

At the turn of the millennium, a considerable number of peace talks greatly helped bring peace to many of the countries, and to date they have enjoyed relative peace and stability as they recover from the wanton destruction that came with civil war. Liberia and Angola in particular have recorded a worthwhile resumption to normalcy, which is highly commendable.

Sudan, which is also in this league, is equally recording a remarkable recovery. But not without a unique set of challenges. The Southern part became semi-autonomous in 2005. The death of John Garang, then vice president of the larger Sudan and leader of the semi-autonomous South Sudan, changed the destiny of South Sudan permanently. The 2010 general elections and the subsequent referendum on secession in 2011 were a good litmus test on the determination of the country to be independent and determine its own future. There have been growing pains, including an unlikely war that killed 10,000 people in December 2013. Famine has ravaged great parts of the country, cattle rustling has been a problem, and illegal firearms are still in the hands of many pastoralists who are the cause of instability in parts of the country.

Illiteracy levels are startling. The poverty levels are equally overwhelming. Oil, which is the lifeblood of our economy, is yet to be fully exploited, given the recurrent problems with Sudan that has seen the pipeline locked down from time to time. Besides, as a landlocked country, our biggest challenge has been finding the right partner with access to the sea or ocean where we can export the crude oil. Kenya and Eritrea

Why South Sudan Matters

are both potential partners, even though both countries are beset by internal problems that render the alternative pipeline to be a pipe dream for now.

Sudan's geographical position made attainment of peace an impossibly difficult task. The neighbouring countries to the west, Chad and Central African Republic, are constantly warring, and the war spills over to Sudan. Ethiopia, Eritrea and Djibouti also had problems that equally affected Sudan in one way or another. Add this to the civil strife that has buffeted Northern Uganda and the problem becomes multifaceted. However, for the past decade, some order has reigned.

It took over twenty years for Sudan to attain a peaceful settlement after the war commenced. And in the two years before the Comprehensive Peace Agreement was signed, war broke out in Darfur. The Darfur war proved to be of genocide proportions and a continuous concern to many governments all over the world.

As South Sudan builds the country from scratch, there is need for a speedy rebuilding and restructuring of the country if we are to catch up with the rest of the world. Of phenomenal importance is the educational system, which lacks harmony and the capacity to make up for the twenty lost years. This means that a whole generation is illiterate, although not necessarily permanently.

The war was devastating, no doubt, and left the education system in shambles. Even prior to the war, the education system was inadequate. To date the national language is English, but the population that has even the mildest grasp of that language is obviously low. This means foreigners still hold a considerably higher number of jobs in the country. After many years of forced *Arabization*, there has been a lack of

Book Two: Introduction

determination to master more than two languages. But with the building of schools this can be changed; the future generations stand to benefit greatly from the investment in education that we make today.

Yet as we move toward the globalization age and South Sudan is resilient and seemingly ready to move on with the world, it is time we paid keen attention to our educational system—a system that will be competitive on a global scale, a system that will readily equip individuals with skills that can be applied everywhere in the world. Hitherto, there lack proper learning structures since many people are still scattered in refugee camps across East Africa as well as the world. Consequently, many young children have been subjected to different curricula. The system needs to be integrated.

It has been my desire to write this book in order to tell my story as a victim of terrorism in the hands of brutal and barbaric Arabs; as a child soldier when I could barely carry a gun; as a refugee in Kenya; and how war has influenced my desire to acquire formal education. I have been fortunate enough to obtain a degree, even though at a more advanced age than most.

It is my hope that by sharing my experience and reflections, I can be an inspiration to the many children who desire to learn.

PART I.
A LEGACY OF WAR

CHAPTER 1
Background

IT IS IMPORTANT TO GIVE A BRIEF HISTORICAL background to the situation in which South Sudan finds itself today. Before separation, Sudan was the largest country in Africa, traversed by the Nile River, the longest river in the world. As I stated previously, it neighbours Ethiopia, and Eritrea to the east; Libya, Central African Republic, and Chad to the west; Kenya, Uganda, and Democratic Republic of Congo to the south; and Egypt to the north.

Contemporary history of Sudan dates as far back as the 18th century when Egypt ruled it from June 1821 until the revolution of Mahdi on January 26, 1885. In this revolution Egyptian forces were evacuated, but during the scramble and

Chapter 1

partition of Africa, Sudan was re-conquered by the Anglo-Egyptian forces in the years 1896–1898. This was followed by an Anglo-Egyptian condominium that was established and ratified in 1936. The British established their colonial rule by the end of World War II and a spirit of Sudan nationalism arose. Two political parties emerged: the National Unionist Party [NUP] led by Ismaelal-Azhari and the Umma Party led by Sayed Sir Abdur-Rahman al-Mahdi. The NUP preferred the union of Sudan and Egypt while the Umma party wanted unqualified independence.

On February 12, 1953, Britain and Egypt granted Sudan self-government and appointed a governor general. Elections were held in December 1953, resulting in an all-Sudanese parliament with NUP emerging victorious, making its leader Ismael al-Azhari Sudan's first prime minister in January 1954.

On August 18, 1955, Equatorial Corps, a military unit composed of the Southerners, mutinied at Torit. Instead of surrendering to the government, they fled and hid with their weapons. This marked the beginning of political instability in Sudan. January 1, 1956, Sudan gained its independence, but although Sudan had eagerly awaited its independence, a cloud of suspicion loomed between the north and the south. Two years later, on November 18, 1958, the country recorded its first ever coup led by General Ibrahim Abboud who seized power from the civilian government. This paved a way for a series of coups and coup attempts. After six months in office, General Abboud squashed another counter-coup on May 22, 1959.

On November 9, 1959, a failed mutiny occurred in Omdurman Infantry School. The government had been

Why South Sudan Matters

rotating in the north all along, but in 1962 civil war in southern Sudan erupted, led by Major General Joseph Lagu of the Anya-Nya I movement, thus setting off what was one of the deadliest civil wars ever recorded in the history of mankind.

With revolts raging in the country, on November 1, 1964, the military regime was abolished and a caretaker committee of civilians was formed under Sir al-Khatim al-Khalifa. Elections followed, and former foreign minister Mohamed Maghoub became the prime minister while NUP leader Ismael al-Azhari, who was the first prime minister, became the president. This, however, did not cure Sudan's woes. There were several coups and attempts at coups. The Anya-Nya I rebel movement in the south expanded its influence and by January 1969, it had contacted foreign countries to obtain support. For instance, Israel trained the Anya-Nya I recruits and shipped weapons to the rebels via Ethiopia and Uganda.

As the government began to shift its focus to the south, a bloodless coup was staged and led by Jaafar Nimeiry, who cited reasons such as civil war in the south, rampant corruption, failure of the country's agricultural policy, and disorganization in civilian party politics.

State House became no bed of roses for Nimeiry, as he had to crush several coup attempts. His leadership came to an end on April 6, 1985. While approaching Cairo International Airport, he got news that he had been toppled. Even though civilian government was restored, it was no remedy for Sudan; on June 30, Prime Minister El-mahdi was toppled by newcomer Lieutenant-General Omar Hassan El-Bashir.

During the Nimeiry regime, some ground had been gained in the south. In 1972, Anya-Nya I movement and the

Chapter 1

government signed the Addis Ababa Peace Agreement and Southern Sudan became a self-governing region. In 1983, John Garang formed the rebel movement known as the Sudan People's Liberation Army [SPLA]. This was the beginning of an intense civil war in the south through which the Southerners demanded political, social, and economic equality. On January 9, 2005, the SPLA and the government signed a Comprehensive Peace Agreement [CPA] that included a permanent ceasefire and accords on sharing wealth and power. The significance of the CPA was reflected in, among other things, swift action by the international community whereby in April 2005 donors pledged 4.5 billion dollars in aid to help the southern part of Sudan recover from the costly civil war.

CHAPTER 2
Underdevelopment (A British Colonial Legacy)

ALMOST ALL AFRICAN COUNTRIES try to shake off the legacies inherited from their colonial periods. The legacies were often strongly entrenched with serving the selfish interests of the colonial masters. And when they left, only a few Africans inherited and used those legacies to their benefit—at the expense of the larger country.

The colonial masters never cared much about the education of the millions of locals. Colonization wasn't intended to do anything other than promote the glory of the Europeans and make the life of the masters as pleasant as possible. This was made possible by those who had to dig in the mines to extract the raw materials, supply cheap labour, and fight in the two world wars.

As Walter Rodney states in his book, *How Europe Underdeveloped Africa*, "The question as to who, and what is responsible for African underdevelopment can be answered at two levels. Firstly, the answer is that the operation of the imperialist system bears major responsibility for African retardation by draining African wealth and by making it impossible to develop more rapidly the resources of the continent. Secondly,

Chapter 2

by those who manipulated the system and those who are either agents or unwittingly accomplices of the said system." This also can be said of the British colonial legacy in Sudan and specifically South Sudan. Britain's fear of the establishment of French influence over the Upper Nile area led to the re-conquest of the Sudan in 1898 as the French were encroaching on Sudan through Southern Sudan. An Anglo-Egyptian force led by General Kitchener invaded Sudan between 1896 and 1898. In 1899, the British and the French concluded an agreement in Europe that made the French pull out of South Sudan, handing over its portion of South Sudan to the same authorities who were already in control of North Sudan.

Between 1898 and 1947, owing to the geographical, political, historical, and cultural differences between North and South Sudan, the British devised a system of separate administration for the two countries. This was to ensure that the effectiveness of the separate administration policy that the British passed, "The Closed Districts Ordinances of 1920s," was achieved. This policy was put in effect after the promulgation of passports and permits in 1922. Every traveler from the two separate regions was required to have them.

After the Immigration Policy came the Language Policy, which stated that English as well as other local languages such as Dinka, Nuer, and Shilluk should be used in the South. Arabic language and customs were utterly rejected. This was done with an intention of totally secluding the South from North. This went as far as the South Sudan colonial Governors and local administrators attending administrative conferences in East Africa.

In contrast, the British created and developed administrative and political structures in the North, using indirect rule whereby they built up authority of different tribal leaders (Nazir and Omda and Sheikh) and cultivated close relationships with religious leaders (descendants of Mahdi and Khatmiyya), families that are still politically important today in Sudan. They also promoted more schooling in the North, such as the Gordon College, and encouraged a growing Sudanese civil service to replace Egyptians. The British thus administered Northern and Southern Sudan as separate colonies.

In a strategy to prepare North Sudan for self-rule, the North Sudan Advisory Council Ordinance was enacted in 1943. It covered all the six North Sudan provinces, comprised of Khartoum, Kordofan, Darfur, Eastern, Northern and Blue Nile provinces. This council was empowered to advise the condominium authority on how to administer North Sudan in certain specific areas. Members of the Advisory Council were all North Sudanese. The ordinance had no application or relevance to the territory of South Sudan despite the fact that the Sudan Elites educated in the West had come in a conference in 1938 to press for one Sudan.

As much as the British had a goodwill intention toward South Sudan, due to the cultural, racial, religious differences, I must say that they failed at a point when they conspired to let the North dominate the South.

The South Sudanese were provoked, having seen that they were not represented in the 1946 Administrative Conference, as resolutions that were passed did not favour them. South Sudanese representatives confirmed the betrayal at the Juba conference of 1947 in which the local chiefs were informed of the irreversibility of the decision to have the

Chapter 2

North rule over the South. This was followed by handpicking thirteen delegates to represent the South in the assembly. Even the Cairo Conference of 1953 was in vain, as out of the 800 administrative posts created to be shared equally between the North and South, only six were given to the South. Thus, when the British gave Sudan internal self-rule, the Northerners were given more powers to rule over the south, opening the doors for recolonisation. Riek Machar has argued that if the British felt and knew that South Sudan was not ready for internal self-rule, it should have handed it over to an international body such as the United Nations, rather than to North Sudan.

Riek Machar goes on to explain that the North Sudanese elites failed to devolve policies that would have consolidated national unity and stability. As a result, Sudan plunged into a continuous state of political, constitutional, economic, and military crisis that lasted more than four decades. Various governments and regimes in Khartoum waged war and denied the South Sudanese equality, social justice, freedom and effective participation in the running of the State.

In the area of education, there has been forced Islamisation and Arabisation of the educational system in the South with the aim to kill indigenous languages and cultures to accentuate Islamic and Arabic dominance.

I say with profound emphasis that the situation in South Sudan as it is now is a result of the British Colonial legacy. If you look back at the dawn of independence, the South was politically marginalized by the North through under-representation, as well as blatant discrimination in cultural, religious, and even academic spheres.

There is an old adage that applies here: "A foreign man

has come and erected a spear in a man's homestead and is busy reigning over the owner's possessions, including his wives." The North virtually choked the Southerners in an openly racist fashion.

The Arabic culture and Islamic values were imposed upon the South in an attempt to do away with their African culture. Moreover, the Southerners have been looked at as the *abeeds* —a derogatory Arabic word for slaves—who did not deserve equal treatment with other citizens of Sudan. You can understand why there has been widespread neglect of socio–economic development in the South.

This is the reason one can justify the nearly half-century bloody civil war. There was a justified desire for the right of self-rule. With a milestone of independence achieved, I am optimistic that the sun has risen from the east and the down-trodden South Sudanese will smile as they bask in its rays. If South Sudan is to be completely liberated, a revolution is what we need—not a bloody revolution, but rather a peaceful, educational revolution. It has been proven time and again that the pen is mightier than the sword.

CHAPTER 3
Education—Not a Priority

WHEN I WAS ELEVEN, the biggest enticement for attending school was the rule that the student who arrived first on Monday morning automatically became the class monitor for the whole week. It was a respected ritual, by far more important than whether we were taught or not. Even community elders paid attention to this trivial practice.

I tried in vain to get to school first on any given Monday for my turn to be the monitor. The school was more than ten kilometres from home, so I, like many pupils, braved the cold at the crack of dawn to get to school. Besides the long distance, the sun at times could be unrelenting, famine was part of life, and there was often no teacher. This made it impossible for us to be interested in formal education. Furthermore, the persistent, raging wars took many male members of the community—some of whom had attended school with me.

Many children of my age were content with shepherding their family cattle. (Like all the Nilotic tribes in sub-Saharan Africa, the Dinka are obsessed with their cattle.) Sometimes during the year when it rained, they fished in seasonal rivers or in swamps that took a long time to drain in the vastly flat South Sudan.

For those who did show up for school, nothing much took place other than the long, interspersed classes and the several hours of play. One chilly Monday morning toward the end of the year, I woke up earlier than usual and asked my mother, Achol Kuel Athian, to prepare me some milk for breakfast.

It was gravely dark, accentuated all the more by the thick, nearly tangible fog that had engulfed our village. My mother was a little hesitant to let me go to school that early. It was too dark and cold, especially for a child of my age. Besides, there were no time restrictions; I could pop in and out of the school at any time. However, my mother did not know that my plan was to be the class monitor that week.

I hurriedly drank my milk, and as soon as some light broke through the fog I hit the road to school. The footpath was deserted since nobody would brave the biting cold to attend to their farm or let their children go to school. It took at least an hour at the outside to get to school. Even at that, I was lucky. Some of my colleagues came as far as twenty kilometres.

On this day, I was the first one to report and could not wait for others to come and crown me their monitor for the coming week. It was not long before the second person arrived and found me seated under the tree that served as our classroom. In our excitement, we decided to climb up the tree and dupe anyone coming that he or she was the first to arrive. Our trick worked. When the ever-punctual Ayien arrived, he was visibly excited at the prospect of being our class prefect for yet another week. But much to his displeasure, his joy was short-lived as we climbed down from the tree to join him.

Soon others came and we huddled ourselves together to ward off the cold. Given that nothing much used to happen at

Chapter 3

school, some of us spent most of the time playing *atuek* while other students went to the forest to forage for fruit. This could go on the whole day, since the teacher hardly ever turned up. And when he did, little or no learning would take place. We only had one teacher who taught the whole school every subject from mathematics to English grammar and science. He mostly came at about midday. This is why we came to school late and nobody cared much.

For many days on end, schooling was treated rather casually and there was a lackadaisical attitude toward knowledge. The country was war-torn and there was never a permanent settlement in the entire northern Bahr el Ghazal State. Many families had run away to escape the all too familiar Arab attacks. Not a single day went by without the sound of a gunshot, and people escaping from their homesteads was the norm. The constant attacks became more ferocious each day.

Still, life in the village was fairly laid-back and mundane; many villagers pursued their daily lives unfettered. As days passed and the war gathered momentum, it became increasingly evident that the male youth in the village must join the army to help in this fight.

Children went to school in the nearby region at either the Catholic Mission or the improvised structures under trees near their homes. The Catholic Mission School was the only institution that provided a comprehensive system of learning to the numerous children whose desire was to go through formal schooling and to hopefully one day be of great benefit to society.

Most of the other schools were based in the village where partially trained teachers tried to teach the children. These schools were basically mud-walled, grass-thatched structures that passed for classrooms. Often the schools lacked chalk or black walls that aid so much in learning. Minimal attention was paid to the welfare of the children who went to such schools to learn. The number of children attending school was dismally low at times and no one was taking charge.

Coming from northern Bahr el Ghazal, which borders northern Sudan, made us all the more vulnerable. The relationship between the Muslim-dominated North and the Christian-dominated South was decidedly sour. The Muslim community generally assumed a superior role and many of the Christians in the South suffered tremendously at their hands. Many young children were brutally forced to learn Arabic and any form of dissent resulted in a savage beating, thus causing them to think of education as a tortuous experience. The fact that the North was insistent on its Arabisation of the South, even forcing their Islam religion on us, was doubly unpopular, making the Southerners hate schooling even more. This brutality angered everyone and if anything, it strengthened the resolve of the South to pursue our freedom relentlessly.

The entire South emigrated in droves to neighbouring countries to seek refuge. That is how loads and loads of South Sudanese citizens ended up in Ethiopia, Uganda, and Kenya. It is here that many resumed their schooling, albeit at more advanced ages compared with Kenyan or Ugandan students.

The late eighties were heady times for South Sudan. The Sudan People's Liberation Army (SPLA) and Sudan People Liberation Movement (SPLM) were intensely training in the forests as the war raged on. They were unrelenting in spite of the overwhelming odds that they faced. The villagers thought that the SPLA soldiers were training to try to stop

Chapter 3

the enemy. (Normally, the soldiers are not in a village to stop the enemy, rather they are there to give the villagers a chance to escape.)

As for the children, we were young and innocent, but even we knew how severe the situation was. As the days passed, it became increasingly dangerous for us to go to school. One by one, many of us abandoned our classes and remained at home to avoid any possible attack at the school. Staying alive became our primary focus.

Our fathers were committed to the cause. The women and children were escorted to Ethiopia or Kenya and the men remained behind to fight the liberation war. My father had been absorbed into the army and my mother, being the first wife of my father, took charge and care of all of us.

Given the sheer size of our polygamous family and without the direction of a man who is normally the breadwinner and responsible for the family security, providing both food and security for us was nearly an insurmountable task for my mother.

CHAPTER 4

My Father's Story

DETAILS ABOUT MY FATHER'S BIRTH border on the mythical. It was commonly said that my grandmother was pregnant for longer than is humanly possible.

"Are you sure, dad?" I once asked him.

In a matter-of-fact manner he said, "Very sure. I had a complete set of teeth and was in every way an old kid when I was born." Later, my Grandmother Aluat confirmed this, but to this day it still sounds incredulous. Maybe it was meant to scare us, by making him a mysterious figure.

The village celebrated his birth. My father was named Malong, which in my community means, "What is on everyone's lips." My father was born in 1963 at a time of numerous challenges; the first secession war had started as soon as Sudan received her independence from Britain. He was born into a war that altogether covered a span of almost 50 years.

As my father grew up in the midst of the war, he had to hunt and gather food for his extended family. My father had a desperate craving to learn foreign languages, mainly Arabic and English. He would nag anyone who came to his home to teach him, and he would be a bother until he learnt a few words or phrases for that day—not the best way to learn a

Chapter 4

new language. The only place one could learn such languages was in Meram, which was countless miles away. Only the businessmen had the luxury of going to Meram, as they had the means to get there. Everyone else had to go through the dense and frightening forest where wild, predatory animals roamed freely. It took three days to get to Meram on foot, and all one had for food was milk that invariably went sour along the way. They would barely be past the second day of their journey when their food ran out.

Luckily for my father, his brother Makuach was old enough and could afford to take him to school. My uncle Makuach was a businessman and he was familiar with the place. He eventually got a one-bedroom house in Meram where my father stayed as he pursued his dream.

My uncle was a mobile trader and operated his business between Warawar and Meram, the two marketing centres. In the meantime, the Arabs had discovered Warawar as a potential market and started trickling down from the north with their goods and services. Giving up was never an option, so my father and uncle had to press on. Whenever their food was scarce, they went into the forest to search for wild food such as fruits, nuts, and berries. These were often hard to come by, given the vastly arid province we live in.

My father joined a school in Meram, where he was taught how to read and write a few Arabic and English words. The school was situated on the site of the Cush people who had been brought there by the Whites. People like my father were regarded as foreigners and were incessantly mistreated.

Nobody was there to care for him. He did a few odd jobs to get some cash for his basic needs as he struggled to fulfil his craving for knowledge. He had problems with the Arabs,

97

so could not befriend them, and life became more complicated each day.

He did eventually learn Arabic and English, which was barely satisfactory as education goes, but as much formal education as anyone would get. Besides, jobs were hardly forthcoming. Sinking into desperation, he had to go back to his village. There were no white-collar jobs there either, and he really longed for one. The only available white-collar job was teaching. The best he could do was try business. Knowing two languages was to his advantage, and he would make a great businessman in either marketing centre: Warawar or Meram.

In Warawar, the inter-clan war had subsided and villagers had taken to the open-air market where they ran small businesses. All communities had started to use the market and it became a forum of interaction for the surrounding communities to exchange goods and services, plus the occasional banter. In the ensuing years of independence, the village warriors had downed their tools to pursue more meaningful ventures that came their way.

Although the country had just achieved independence and had considerable exposure to the foreigners, the locals were never ready to let go of their pre-colonial life. For instance, my father tells me that back then men made a name for themselves in wrestling matches, and he had trounced many of his peers. Also, men had to wrestle men from other clans before they were allowed to marry a woman from that clan.

It seemed to my father that the Arabs had taken over Warawar. They were the elders in the local market and their numbers kept increasing. Soon they wanted to rule and they appointed one of their own as Market Chief Organizer (the head of the market). That is when all hell broke loose. The

Chapter 4

locals were suddenly aware that the market had been taken over by the Arabs and they resisted. The scene was unprecedented. The town was in chaos—people huddled in small groups, furtively whispering. There was a feeling of malevolence in the air, and rumours of war were rife.

The town was closed down for several days. The traders mourned their losses. The people were forced to return to the primitive practice of barter trade. Signs of the markets reopening any time soon were fewer and fewer with each passing day. War was looming—the peace they had enjoyed was about to come to an abrupt end.

My father married at the age of seventeen, at the outbreak of the Anyanya II war in the early 1980s. My mother gave birth to their firstborn, Anei Malong, and I was born in 1984, the following year, at the break of dawn on a very cold morning. (Please understand that in a country constantly at war, there are no hospitals, no birth records, so all dates of birth are approximate.) My mother had been helped during my birth by her mother-in-law, who was partially blind. Getting a qualified medical practitioner to conduct the whole process was difficult, but the midwives had perfected this job. One midwife and a witch doctor assisted on that exceedingly cold morning, ushering me into a full-scale war that had brought immeasurable destruction and loss of life. And that was just the beginning.

Prior to the war, those in the Fagar, the Central Equatorial region where we lived, had sensed that war was imminent. At the time, my father was running a clandestine business with the Arabs. This mainly involved the exchange of our cattle for Arab guns. The arms trade had become commonplace and the number of arms my father secured had increased greatly. This exchange went on until someone realized what was going on, and my father became the most wanted person by the council of Arab elders.

It had never occurred to anyone that there could ever be war in the "Garden of Eden," as we used to call our home village; the expression obviously borrowed from the Catholic teachings in the nearby church. The top leaders like Garang Mabior were not in the country at this point, and there was a lack of coherent leadership. My father prepared to leave, along with his followers of predominantly young men willing to fight for a cause they believed in. He had ensured that everyone had a gun and enough bullets to sustain themselves throughout the fighting period. However, the guns were intended mainly for self-defence.

As they advanced to the northeast of Sudan, they came across Garang Mabior's troops. They joined forces with them, as they had the same vision—to conquer the enemy that was hell-bent on chasing the local people out of their native land. In one large troop, they went to Ethiopia for military training with the Anyanya II troops. They were the first troops to train for the war, and they were going to be away for a while. My father was the troop leader.

(*At this writing, my father is the Army General Chief of Staff of the Sudan People's Liberation Army, and former Governor of Bahr el Ghazal state.*)

Chapter 4

As my mother recounts, the Arabs struck a day after I was born. Before breakfast that morning, those in the house heard a blast, certainly from a gunshot within the compound. They went outside to look, only to see the air filled with dust as horsemen rode into the market and shot villagers.

What they witnessed was inconceivable. It had taken the forefathers thousands of years to establish the Warawar as a vibrant trading centre, but within minutes, the centre was destroyed. The villagers were chased from their homes; houses were burnt and homes shattered. Many fled to seek refuge in far-off places. Their hopes that the war would not last were dashed—it was nearly three decades before these people were able to return to their homes.

There are few, if any, reasons to smile or find any humor whatsoever when one is subjected to constant war, but this story told to me by my mother comes close. In a far-off corner of the village where probably the largest grass-thatched house and the largest home brewing centre in the whole of Sudan existed, some drunkards went on about their business of drinking, ignorantly unaware that war had come to their village These men were known to praise the local brew, popularly referred to as "mou," as in "it is more than life," saying that it neutralised all the stress in the world and made the burdens light. In their dreamy state, while regaling each other with their stale jokes, the attackers were approaching. Three of the men had not yet drunk their fill, and realised what was going on in the village. They, along with the brewer, took to their heels, leaving the remaining two men utterly absorbed in the local brew. When the others escaped, they drunkenly dismissed them as cowards and went on drinking as if nothing was happening. Although they did

take turns as lookouts—when one was keeping watch the other was drinking, and so on. They drank from a straw extracted from a local shrub. It was long and coiled, which made the experience all the more worthwhile.

When it came time for the one who had been on watch to take his turn with the brew, it was empty. A fight ensued, but it was short-lived. They merely went to the big drums to draw some more mou.

The Arabs approached the house with their guns cocked. They saw the two men chatting and drinking as if in defiance to their encroachment. The drunkards somehow sensed that they were in danger, and then realised that their spy hole had been obscured. They knew that they were in danger. They started to leave the house, but in their haste knocked over a heavy pot and lost their balance. One of them fell on top of the other, and instead of fleeing, they started punching each other. The Arabs watched, amused. They were sure that by the end of their fight they would be exhausted and easier to deal with. The Arabs soon lost interest in the fight and were watching their backs, on the lookout for a possible attack since they were now in a war zone area. They were sure that the locals would try to retaliate. But it had been hours since the latest attack, and all the villagers had deserted the village. The weapons the Arabs had used were too powerful compared to theirs.

The two drunken men had sobered up enough to realize what was happening, but pretended to continue their fight until they were sure that the Arabs weren't watching, then they escaped through the window and vanished into the forest. When the Arabs discovered what had happened, they started shooting randomly into the forest, hoping that the bullets would randomly hit one or both of them.

Chapter 4

There were some who tried to resist the attackers in their own small way. My grandfather Awan Anei, my father's father, was one such person. I'm told he was an extremely daring character. His courage, more often than not, bordered on misplaced heroism. He killed anyone who crossed his garden. But this time it was warranted. Reportedly, he fought the attackers single-handed, and eluded them for more than five hours. He was not going to let the attackers chase him off his valued piece of ancestral land. This was in 1960, and he passed away in 1965.

All over the world, there are those who are ever ready to cash in on a crisis—who have access to basic needs in time of war and will sell them at absurdly exploitative prices. These people are usually ready to do anything for cash, including kidnapping and demanding a king's ransom. They are equally capable of handing over anyone to captors for a fee. My grandfather was eventually captured by a fellow villager who *sold* him to the enemy. This was a welcome relief to the Arabs, because he vigorously opposed their occupation, and they perceived him as their archenemy. They sent him to Malualkon, a town south of our hometown, where he was jailed and starved to death. By the time the villagers came from their hiding places, their freedom fighter, my grandfather, was no more.

CHAPTER 5
Exodus to Ethiopia

ONE DAY AS WE CHILDREN WERE PLAYING in the school-yard, we heard loud gunshots coming from the nearby Konchibek estate. Our playing came to a sudden stop. We used to live in the Konchibek region and we were worried that our home was no more. As the gunshots grew even more deafening, we thought it was possible that the SPLA was returning fire on the attackers from the North.

These attacks from the North were relentless. The attackers would often kidnap children from schools and kill others who could not walk long distances. This day we had time to run as far as our feet could take us. Santino Muong, my closest friend, and I were the youngest, only around five years old, and we just could not keep up the pace. We were left behind. I realized that I was lagging even farther behind Santino when the distance between us widened. Suddenly I felt a numbing feeling. My feet could not carry me anymore. I looked down and saw blood flowing profusely from my left foot. I had been shot, but in the confusion had not felt it. The pain was excruciating, and there was no one in sight to help me. For a brief moment I thought of my mother, who was ever ready to help even a stranger.

My fears were heightened by the fact that as soon as gov-

Chapter 5

ernment soldiers from the North discovered me in the bush, they would slaughter me like a chicken, without mercy. With this in mind, I gathered all my will power, grabbed a firm wooden stick that was nearby, and lifted myself up. I dragged myself through the bush, avoiding the pathway where I might run into the soldiers.

Luckily for me, one of the escaping villagers came across me and saw that I was injured. This good man chose not to selfishly run away. Instead, he supported me while I limped deep into the forest.

Meanwhile, I was cursing myself for not having listened to my mother earlier that day when she told me not to go to school. There was a local proverb, *"meth chi kin maan ku hun ping abithou kangong.* Loosely translated that means, "A child who does not listen to his mother or father's advice dies poor."

My gunshot wound was the price of an education in South Sudan at that time, but I was not the only victim—many of my friends lost their arms or legs.

We were a group of young boys trying to survive when we heard of news from the next village, Malualkon, that there was soldier training in Ethiopia for the Southerners who were in a desperate situation. It came down to a choice of death, accepting Islamic force, or going to Ethiopia to be trained to defend ourselves. I was taken to Ethiopia to be trained as a child soldier. It would be four years before I would see my mother again.

On a day after returning to my home from soldier training, I stood outside admiring the various clothes that the Arabians were wearing, while at the same time mentally cursing their war. Then I saw an expectant woman sobbing uncontrollably. She seemed to be in excruciating pain and I could tell, even in my naiveté that she was apparently on her labour pains. Her abdomen was swollen like a weaverbird's nest and she seemed ready to burst open. She was in agony, and begging for help.

People were too occupied by their own troubles to care about her, and no one seemed inclined to help. It appeared that every step she took was insufferably painful, and then she stopped trying to move at all. An idea struck my mind. I knew of an old woman who was a midwife, but only did so at her homestead, which was a stone's throw away from the marketplace. I had to be quick, lest the pregnant woman lose her life and the baby.

By the time I made my way back from seeing the old woman, I was relieved to learn that Good Samaritans had helped the woman and saved her life and that of the boy child she had given birth to. The child was weak and blissfully unaware of the war that was all around him. I sighed in relief that the delivery was successful. The child was named Garang Atem.

That day's weather had been bright and deceptively friendly, but within a few hours it grew gloomy and foggy. When the weather changed abruptly like this, it was particularly ominous for the Cush people. They worried about the Arabs, who seemed invincible and ready to pounce on their land. In recent years, the Arabs had been encroaching upon their land, and were now on the verge of taking it over forcefully.

Gunshots had become a part of our lives. Smoke was rapidly gathering. The marketplace that had temporarily resumed business had been attacked again and people ran for

Chapter 5

their lives. There seemed to be no end to the gunfire; the Arabs were ruthless. The black Africans occupying the region were better off packing and leaving the place, given they were outnumbered, outgunned, and outmuscled. The market was engulfed in smoke, and destruction this time was irreparable. The message from the Arabs was, Leave or we shall annihilate you.

I turned to the left and saw that the woman who had just given birth hours earlier was abandoned. She clung to her baby as though their lives were going to end at any moment. I gathered courage amid the violent turn of events and grabbed the child, holding him close to my body, and held the hand of the mother as we took off as fast as we could manage. The mother was completely worn-down, so we had to go at a slower, more dangerous pace.

Everywhere we ran there was noise. The old and the young seemed to be crying in perfect symphony. Their cries were directed to the sky and from wherever they thought help would come. The whole village was on fire. The granaries were burned, and the villagers watched helplessly as their grass-thatched houses were torched and burned to the ground. The Arabs were riding very strong and powerful horses, using all kinds of weapons, modern and old, to hack the villagers or shoot them at random. The livestock was driven away as the surviving villagers disappeared into the bush.

The destruction was unfathomable. As the British philosopher Thomas Hobbes said, force and fraud are the two cardinal virtues in war. For me, I thought life had come to an end. What a waste. What a misery. Where were our leaders? Where were the parents? I longed for a weapon to take to the battlefield. So many questions and so few answers.

Why South Sudan Matters

By the time I was seven years old I had intermittently attended school up to class three. Even with the interruptions and the circumstances under which we lived, I was considerably luckier than most. However, moving out of Sudan was unavoidable, as life there proved indefensible. Our first natural choice of destination was Ethiopia. My father had left as soon as I was born to fight for the South. I was with my mother and other women who were in a similar situation.

Moving to Ethiopia was comparable to the biblical exodus. There were thousands of us migrating to escape certain death. The comparison with the biblical exodus doesn't stop here; at the time we were living in Central Equatorial, which is over five hundred miles from Ethiopia. We walked all the hundreds of miles to Ethiopia under the inspiration of the late Dr. John Garang, the SPLM leader at the time. I had met him at a place in the middle of a forest named New Site so the enemy would not know the exact location. We were the first to settle there. When he addressed us he said, "We belong here and we will live with those who need us. We will fight for our freedom. We are not Muslims and we will not be forced to be Muslims." He never failed to say, "With freedom, there is enough food and clothes, and we will soon be free." There was shouting and clapping and joy once again as he said the words we wanted to hear. We were fighting and surviving on our own, but we believed that we served under Dr. John Garang—for whoever was not with him, was against him.

We took the longest route to Ethiopia; more circuitous than diametrical, for reasons to date I have never compre-

Chapter 5

hended. For many days, we dwelt in the thick equatorial forest that could be frightening—especially at night.

Worry and concern was written all over the faces of the adults, but as children, our blissful ignorance of the grave situation saved us from the mental agony the adults were suffering. They were constantly on the lookout for any possible attack. The attacks had become constant, and death an almost normal occurrence.

Since the commencement of the war, and before our exodus to Ethiopia, my mother had settled in the forest with her two children; my brother, who was only a year older, and me. She was not afraid of the wild animals that could tear us apart at any time. Yet it was next to impossible for my mother to take care of us. She had to be mama and papa for her two demanding boys. She went through grueling hardships trying to fend for us. She was not alone in the ongoing distress. Many women whose husbands had left were faced with the same ordeal. Our houses as well as the granaries had been burnt by the Arabs, so there was no food. We survived on providence.

The overall feeling was one of gloom. Many villagers were worried about where they would get food until the next season, and that was only if they were able to plant in peace or live to see another day. The Arabs had damaged the morale of the villagers terribly. Life had lost meaning. No relief was forthcoming. The war was only beginning; it was going to be a long time before this could be considered a humanitarian issue and we could qualify for relief food.

For my mother, and indeed for many women, it was a different story. The husband was away trying to fight for the black people of South Sudan. The wife was finding her way through the Amommom (pronounced as Hong *Amummum*) forest. Amommom was one of the most dangerous forests in all of Southern Sudan. Those who went there rarely survived. And if they did somehow make it back, they were forever traumatized.

On the horribly difficult journey to Ethiopia, it was by a sheer stroke of luck that my mother ran into Uncle Angany Wal and his family. They and another man among the exiled gave us a welcome feeling of security and safety.

The forest we had been living in was to be the home of the displaced South Sudanese for the next several years. They had no way of knowing whether it was safe back in the village.

CHAPTER 6
Starting Over in Kenya

IN SEPTEMBER OF 1998, I AGAIN LEFT MY MOTHER—this time to pursue an education in Kenya.

We arrived just a month after the terrorists had bombed the then American Embassy and the nearby Cooperative House, killing more than two hundred people. At the time, the country was reeling from the effects of the unthinkable terrorist attack.

This was the first bombing of such magnitude to rock the city centre of any East Africa capital. It was the main topic of conversation everywhere we went.

This was contrary to our expectations. We had escaped Ethiopia to ensure that our learning was not interrupted. Our stay there ended after war broke in the Ethiopia-Eritrean border, plunging the whole country into a war. Our lives were in jeopardy, and furthering our studies was out of the question. We would have gone back to Sudan, but the war in Sudan was not about to end any time soon.

Our coming to Kenya was inspired by the peaceful nature of the country, even though it was surrounded by perpetually warring nations. The disturbing news upon our arrival that Kenya was now a susceptible target of terrorists was not the reception we were anticipating. Coming from a country that

Why South Sudan Matters

had been embroiled in war, this was reason enough to be pessimistic. The northern part of Kenya was not as stable as the occupied southern part was. A number of Sudanese citizens had settled in refugee camps in the north, and a number of children were already attending school.

I initially settled at Kapenguria, the capital of West Pokot County where I lived with my stepmother Nyantony Awar and six of my siblings. I tentatively began my schooling and after several false starts, at last there was light at the end of the academic tunnel. Arrangements were made for me to start at class three. I was fifteen going on sixteen, tall and lean. I would later become notorious in the school for being the oldest pupil. In Kenya, by the age of fifteen many pupils are through with primary schooling and already in secondary school. Thus it was extremely embarrassing in my initial days, and I was the butt of many jokes. My peers were no more than ten years old, mean-spirited (as only children can be), and had a sense of belonging and entitlement. In addition, I didn't know the two common languages in Kenya; Swahili and English. This was monumentally embarrassing, given that many children derived extreme pleasure in my shaky command of the language.

Reading a passage in class was a problem. Many teachers insisted on the random reading of passages, and those impudent children eagerly awaited my turn. Of course I got all the pronunciations wrong, much to the entertainment of my peers.

My life was often complicated by teachers when they insisted that I clean the black wall, because of my height. It was never a fun experience, no matter how much my fellow pupils celebrated it. I will never know whether it was because

Chapter 6

of my height or because the teachers derived pleasure from my embarrassment.

Another thing I found difficult was that the teachers in Kenya attended classes unfailingly. This was a far cry from life in Sudan or even in Ethiopia where school was treated as casually as a market. Dealing with the pressure was no easy task. After the many years of languid schooling in my country and Ethiopia, I found it hard to cope with the seriousness with which the teachers conducted their business.

But of all the odds, the most difficult to overcome was the language barrier. No one seemed to be in a position to help me learn a little Swahili or English in order for me to communicate. With Kiswahili being the official language of Kenya, most children, especially around urban centres, master it by the age of ten. It took me almost a year to have a firm grasp of Swahili, but this greatly helped me communicate with the locals. Henceforth, no one could insult me or gossip about me within my earshot. This greatly boosted my confidence and helped me associate with the other pupils better. I could argue my case, I could complain against unfair treatment, and most important, I could be heard. However, my class performance was still low. My grades were not in the least impressive. Although I consoled myself in the fact that no parental authority was directly overseeing my performance, I knew that at the end of the day the results were going to affect me directly. I worked desperately hard to change things, but it was not paying off fast enough.

The teachers encouraged me, and my guardians were patient with me, as much as any understanding parents would be. Having gone through three completely different systems, it was quite confusing. My advanced age complicated matters further, since I could not imagine wasting another year. It was a common phenomenon in Kenya that those who were behind in class had to go through the system all over again. Sometimes a student could be in a class for up to four years. It was a daunting prospect, yet as every day dawned, it seemed to be more of a possibility. I was determined to improve my grades to ensure that my learning was not delayed or interrupted. This called for intense self-discipline. I avoided all bad company, determined not to repeat even a single class. Many of the children got used to my age and some even went a step further to allow me the necessary respect that we all accord those older than we are. I could sense the vicarious sympathy among the pupils as well as the teachers, who encouraged me to work harder. It was almost two years before I could fully grasp the academic system and my performance picked up.

I familiarized myself with the Kenyan system and adapting became easier. There weren't many distractions, such as the sporadic wars that interrupted the learning in Sudan and Ethiopia. Instability, common in Sudan, kept many children out of school. Even to date, several years after the signing of the Comprehensive Peace Agreement (CPA), many such children who are now adults have never stepped into a classroom.

Many of the Sudanese children with me in Kenya grappled with my same problems, and often shared with me their fears and aspirations. Their primary goal was to get a grip on the queen's language and a little Swahili to help solve the communication problems. For most of them, they longed for the resumption of peace in Sudan so they could go back and help rebuild the country.

Life in Kenya was generally good. There were not many

Chapter 6

upheavals in the region. At least the days were defined, and we all looked forward to a brighter day. We had access to food and education, unlike in Sudan where these things were luxuries. We could access health facilities, and the housing system was good enough compared to the life in Sudan where living in the forest was often the only option following the constant raids.

While we felt no hostility in Kenya whatsoever, the yearning for "home sweet home" never left us.

PART II.
CHILDREN AT WAR

CHAPTER 7

The Reprehensible Side of War

IN AFRICA, IT IS ESTIMATED THAT UP TO 120,000 children are currently used as combatants or support personnel, representing 40 percent of the worldwide total of possibly 300,000 children in regular and irregular armed forces. Africa has the highest growth rate in the use of children in conflict, and on average, the age of those enlisted is decreasing.

According to Olara Otunnu, former Under-Secretary-General of the United Nations and Special Representative for Children and Armed Conflict, "Today's warfare especially the exploitation, abuse and use of children are nothing short

Chapter 7

of a process of self-destruction. This isn't a small matter. This goes to the very heart of whether or not there is the promise of a future for these societies."

Military recruitment is not only harmful to the children themselves but to societies as a whole. Children's lost years of schooling reduce societies' human and economic development potential. Many child soldiers grow up physically and psychologically scarred and prone to violence, increasing the danger of future cycles of conflict and damaging the chances of peaceful, stable democracy that are demonstrably linked to human and social well-being.

In addition to the obvious risks to children of participation in armed conflict—which apply equally to adults—children are often at an added disadvantage as combatants. Their immaturity may lead them to take excessive risks. According to one rebel commander in the Democratic Republic of Congo, "[children] make good fighters because they're young and want to show off. They think it's all a game, so they're fearless." Moreover, and as a result of being widely perceived to be dispensable commodities, they tend to receive little or no training before being thrust into the front line. Reports from Burundi and Congo-Brazzaville suggest that they are often massacred in combat as a result.

Children may begin participating in conflict from as young as the age of seven. Some start as porters (carrying food or ammunition) or messengers, others as spies. One rebel commander declared, "They're very good at getting information. You can send them across enemy lines and nobody suspects them because they're so young." And as soon as they are strong enough to handle an assault rifle or a semi-automatic weapon (normally at 10 years of age), children are used as soldiers. One former child soldier from Burundi stated, *"We spent sleepless nights watching for the enemy. My first role was to carry a torch for grown-up rebels. Later I was shown how to use hand grenades. Barely within a month or so, I was carrying an AK-47 rifle or even a G3."*

When they are not actively engaged in combat, they can often be seen manning checkpoints; adult soldiers can normally be seen standing 15 metres behind the barrier so that if bullets start flying, it is the children who are the first victims. And in any given conflict when even a few children are involved as soldiers, all children, civilian or combatant, come under suspicion. A military sweep in Congo-Brazzaville, for instance, killed all rebels who had attained the age of bearing arms.

Atrocities have all too frequently been committed by child soldiers, sometimes under the influence of drugs or alcohol, which they may be forced to take. In Sierra Leone, for example, a journalist from the French newspaper *Le Figaro* claimed that most of the rebels are children no older than 14 who are under the effect of drugs and alcohol. He reported what one of them told him about torture they inflict on their victims:

> *"At two p.m., they gouge out two eyes, at three p.m., they cut off one hand, at four p.m., they cut off two hands, at five p.m., they cut off one foot and . . . at seven p.m. it is the dead body which falls down."*

But drugs alone do not account for the atrocities committed by children. It is their systematic abuse by adults, combined with a pervasive culture of violence that is ultimately responsible. In March 1998, at the trial of a 13-year-old

Chapter 7

Democratic Republic of the Congo soldier who had shot and killed a local Red Cross volunteer in Kinshasa after a dispute on a football pitch, even the prosecution declared that the lack of control of boy soldiers was as much the fault of their older commanders and constituted extenuating circumstances. The boy was nonetheless condemned to death, although President Kabila later commuted the sentence to life imprisonment.

Though child soldiers have committed and continue to commit some terrible crimes in wartime, they are still entitled, as children, to special provision and protection. Somehow, the differing needs for justice and the reintegration in society of former child soldiers have to be accommodated. Children of sufficient age to be charged with criminal responsibility demand special procedures to take account of their youth and developmental state, while those under the age of criminal responsibility require appropriate measures to promote their psychological recovery and social reintegration.

Per former UNICEF executive director Carol Bellamy, "Children are not expendable. "They belong in schools and in their families. It is our responsibility to ensure that they are protected from the horrors of warfare."

Note: The information above and in some other parts of Part II are from a report by Stuart Maslen, Coordinator of the Coalition to Stop the Use of Child Soldiers. The research was coordinated by Joël Mermet, and was produced by Françoise Jaffré, Communication Officer of the Coalition. The full report can be read online at: http://reliefweb.int/sites/relief web.int/files/resources/C157333FCA91F573C1256C13 0033E448-chilsold.htm

CHAPTER 8

Girls at Greater Risk

GIRLS—ESPECIALLY ORPHANS OR UNACCOMPANIED girls —are especially vulnerable because they are often sexually exploited, raped or otherwise abused, subjected to human trafficking and prostitution, and forced to be "wives" by other combatants. This, in turn, can result in physical and psychological trauma, unwanted pregnancies, sexually transmitted diseases (including HIV/AIDS), and social stigmatization.

In case studies from El Salvador, Ethiopia, and Uganda, the Coalition to Stop the Use of Child Soldiers has estimated that up to one-third of child soldiers in these countries were girls.

In most of the armed conflicts in Africa, girls are recruited by coercion (Angola, Uganda, and Sierra Leone) and, although most girl soldiers are found in opposition groups, there are some government armed forces that recruit them. Their special needs are rarely provided for in disarmament, demobilisation, and reintegration (DDR) programs.

The particular needs of female child soldiers were emphasised in UN Security Council Resolution 1325, adopted in 2000. This resolution reaffirmed that the international community had to pay special attention to the particular vulnerability of women during war, given the appalling nature of

Chapter 8

systematic sexual abuse and the use of rape as a weapon of war in some modern conflicts.

In recent years, the International Criminal Tribunals for Rwanda and the former Yugoslavia (ICTR and ICTY) have successfully prosecuted people for sexual violence and rape. Impunity for such crimes should be further eradicated over time with the inclusion of grave forms of sexual violence (including rape, sexual slavery, and enforced prostitution) as war crimes that fall within the jurisdiction of the International Criminal Court (ICC).

Like many males, females joined one of the factions in war for their own protection. Unwillingly, they became the girlfriends or wives of rebel leaders or members: "Wartime women" is the term they themselves use.

Concy A. a 14-year old girl, was abducted from Kitgum in Uganda and taken to Sudan by a violent rebel group, the LRA (Lord's Resistance Army.) *"In Sudan we were distributed to men and I was given to a man who had just killed his woman. I was not given a gun, but I helped in the abductions and grabbing of food from villagers. Girls who refused to become LRA wives were killed in front of us to serve as a warning to the rest of us."* The risks to these girls of sexually transmitted diseases or unwanted pregnancies are enormous.

Grace A. gave birth on open ground to a baby girl fathered by one of her LRA rebel abductors. Then she was forced to continue fighting. *"I picked up a gun and strapped the baby on my back. But we were defeated by government forces, and I found a way to escape."*

Girls are also the victims of child soldiers. In Algeria, a young woman from one of the villages where massacres had taken place said that all of the killers were boys under 17.

Why South Sudan Matters

Some boys who looked to be around 12 decapitated a 15-year-old girl and played "catch" with the head.

http://reliefweb.int/sites/reliefweb.int/files/resources/C157333FCA 91F573C1256C130033E448-chilsold.htm

CHAPTER 9
Recruitment of Children

Governmental Armed Forces

If domestic legislation regarding minimum age of recruits were respected in practice, the problem of child soldiers in Africa would be significantly reduced. However, given the lack of systematic birth registration, younger children are inevitably recruited even if the will to prevent underage recruitment exists. Many African States appear to follow appropriate recruitment procedures of a minimum age of 18, but others do not—some recruit children no more than 7 or 8 years of age almost as a matter of course. Some children do volunteer to join the armed forces (though the true number will vary depending on how one interprets the word volunteer). In the Democratic Republic of the Congo, for example, between 4,000 and 5,000 adolescents responded to a radio broadcast calling (in clear violation of international law) for 12- to 20-year-olds to enroll to defend their country. Most were street children.

Tens of thousands of children are forced to join up, sometimes at gunpoint. In Angola, forced recruitment of youth (*Rusgas*) continues in some of the suburbs around the capital and throughout the country, especially in rural areas. It has been claimed that military commanders have paid police offi-cers to find new recruits and Namibia has collaborated with Angola in catching Angolans who have fled to Namibia to avoid conscription. In Eritrea, a 17-year-old Ethiopian pris-oner of war interviewed by a British journalist claimed that he was playing football in Gondar High School when Ethiopian government soldiers rounded up 60 boys and sent them to a military training camp. In Uganda, there have been persistent reports that street children in Kampala have been approached by soldiers and forced to join the army in order to be sent to the Democratic Republic of Congo.

Military Schools

In a number of African countries, military schools serve to give children an education, not just as a backdoor form of underage recruitment. In Benin, for example, the *Centre National d'Instruction des Forces Armées* educates children from the age of 13 and the *Prytanée militaire* of Bembereke selects children of high ability from the 6th grade. Children in these schools are not members of the armed forces and they are encouraged, but not forced, to pursue a military career after graduation, which usually occurs when they are about 19 or 20 years of age. In other countries, such as Burundi and Rwanda, military schools appear to serve as backdoor recruit-ment into the armed forces of tens of thousands of children.

Opposition Groups

In situations of armed conflict, wherever governments have recruited and used children as soldiers, so have armed oppo-

Chapter 9

sition groups, and just as certain African governments have chosen to violate national laws, so opposition groups have flouted public declarations and pledges not to recruit and use children in combat. More often, however, no such declaration has been made. The Hutu opposition in Burundi has systematically recruited boys and girls under 15 years of age into its armed groups; and a number of different sources have stated that the Front for the Liberation of the Cabinda Enclave (FLEC-FAC) in Angola also recruited children into their forces. The FLEC-FAC was reported to have children as young as eight years of age among its ranks and an estimated 30–40 per cent of them were girls. In Sierra Leone, reports have clearly detailed the fact that rebel forces recruit children below 18 years of age and demonstrate that children as young as five are enrolled.

In Uganda, the Lord's Resistance Army (LRA) systematically abducts children from their schools, communities, and homes. Children who attempt to escape, resist, cannot keep up, or become ill are killed. Generally, the rebels take their captives across the border to an LRA camp in Sudan. There, these children are tortured, threatened, and sexually abused. Latest reports suggest that the LRA has now turned to selling abducted children into slavery in exchange for arms.

Children enrolled by force into armed opposition groups often have little choice but to remain and fight. In Uganda, for example, if children abducted by the LRA do manage to escape or surrender, they may face the wrath of the Government. Despite claims made on Ugandan television by the armed forces that they are *"rescuing these children daily,"* and *"handing them to charity organisations for care,"* in January 1999, the Ugandan army executed, in circumstances to be

125

clarified, five teenage boys between the ages of 14 and 17 suspected of being rebel soldiers. Moreover, in April 1998, 25 boys were charged with treason. All these boys faced the death sentence even though they were *abducted* by rebels and used as child soldiers by them. The children were charged with failing to release information about rebel soldiers or are said to have fought with the rebels. The death penalty in these cases would be a manifest violation of the Geneva Conventions and their Additional Protocols and of the Convention on the Rights of the Child. These international treaties, to which Uganda is a party, clearly prohibit capital punishment for those under 18 years of age at the time of the commission of the offence.

But even some of those armed opposition groups who use children as soldiers recognise the dangers. *"It's true they can hold a gun and fight, but you spoil the education of a child,"* Songolo [a rebel commander in the Democratic Republic of Congo] said, adding that he is against the practice but has seen many child soldiers in the country. *"Their minds go bad . . . they become criminals if they leave."* (This of course applies as much to volunteers as it does to conscripts.) Indeed, there are reports that the Sudan People's Liberation Army (SPLA), which has used many thousands of children in their struggle against the regime in Khartoum, is finally realising that they have created a generation of children who cannot read or write and know only the respect that is earned by the barrel of a gun. It remains to be seen whether they are truly willing to stop recruiting children and to demobilise those that are currently serving in their ranks.

http://reliefweb.int/sites/reliefweb.int/files/resources/C157333FCA 91F573C1256C130033E448-chilsold.htm

CHAPTER 10

Can Anything Be Done?

THERE IS RECENT PROGRESS DESPITE THE ODDS. Africa Check is a nonprofit organisation set up in 2012 to promote accuracy in public debate and the media in Africa. The goal of their work is to raise the quality of information available to society across the continent. The following is from a report researched by Shirley de Villiers:

> The year 2014 was a "devastating" one for children in armed conflicts, according to the United Nations Children's Fund (UNICEF).
>
> Worldwide, 230 million children lived in countries affected by armed conflicts; 15 million were caught up in violent conflicts in countries such as the Central African republic (CAR) and South Sudan; hundreds were kidnapped; and tens of thousands were recruited or used by government forces and armed groups.
>
> The recruitment and use of children by armed groups is one of "six grave violations" against children identified by the United Nations Security Council. Yet the practice is pervasive, despite various legal instruments that aim to protect the rights of children in conflict.

Who is a child soldier?

A child associated with a government force or armed group is "any person below 18 years of age who has been recruited or used by an armed group in any capacity, including but not limited to children, boys and girls, used as fighters, cooks, porters, messengers, spies or for sexual purposes." This is according to the Paris Principles and Guidelines on Children Associated with Armed Forces or Armed Groups, an agreement reached at a 2007 conference on children in armed conflict hosted by the French government and UNICEF.

Child soldiers are often forcibly conscripted through coercion, abduction, and threat. Others voluntarily enlist in armed groups.

However, the office of the special representative of the UN secretary-general for children and armed conflict noted that "voluntary enlistment" is something of a misnomer. Children present themselves to join armed groups in "a desperate attempt to survive" and escape poverty and insecurity.

How many child soldiers are there?

Accurate figures pertaining to child soldiers around the world are difficult to come by. A child protection specialist at UNICEF, Ibrahim Sesay, told Africa Check that a lack of access to territories under the control of armed groups and the difficulty of determining the age of children who do not have birth certificates hampers research.

However, UNICEF does undertake assessments in states and communities affected by conflict. "The number of children recruited and embedded within the command structures of armed forces or armed groups are based on estimates per geographic location," Sesay said.

Chapter 10

Information is drawn from various sources, including informants, armed forces, and armed groups. Data is then aggregated and triangulated (confirmed by more than one method of data collection) to assess validity and consistency.

In 2007, UNICEF estimated 250,000 children were active in armed forces across the world. UNICEF does not have current estimates of the total number of child soldiers around the world and in Africa. A breakdown will only be available once research is completed next year.

However, Sesay said their research points to "tens of thousands" of child soldiers around the world, with 12,000 children currently used by armed forces and groups in South Sudan and 10,00 recruited in the Central African Republic (CAR) in 2014.

What is being done to end the use of child soldiers?

Various international groups, such as Child Soldiers International, War Child, and the International Rescue Committee, work to eliminate the use of child soldiers. This is done through research, monitoring, advocacy and policy development, or through grassroots work with former combatants.

The UN started monitoring and reporting on violations against children in armed conflict in 2005, when the Security Council mandated it. In accordance with this, the secretary general provides an annual report on children in armed conflict, as well as country-specific reports.

The monitoring mechanism was put in place to ensure children are protected in line with international legal benchmarks. The most recent of these include the Optional Protocol on the Convention of the Rights of the Child and the Rome Statute.

The UN's Optional Protocol on Children in Armed Conflict, which entered into force in 2002, obligates signatories to raise the age of voluntary recruitment from 15 years, and sets the benchmark for compulsory recruitment by states and participation in hostilities at 18 years. It also forbids non-state armed groups from recruiting or using children under the age of 18.

The Rome Statute, which created the International Criminal Court (ICC) and also entered into force in 2002, sets another benchmark by making it a war crime to conscript or enlist children under the age of 15, or have them participate in hostilities.

In December 2014, the former commander-in-chief of the Forces Patriotiques pour la Liberation du Congo (FPLC) in the Democratic Republic of Congo (DRC) became the first person to be convicted of the crime by the ICC. Thomas Lubanga DYilo was sentenced to 14 years of imprisonment.

The UN launched the Children, Not Soldiers campaign last year to end the recruitment and use of child soldiers in government forces by 2016. Countries of concern include the DRC, Somalia, South Sudan, and Sudan, as well as Afghanistan, Myanmar, and Yemen.

How is Africa faring?

The UN secretary-general's 2015 report on children in armed conflict listed 57 parties that recruited or used children in armed conflict last year. These included 29 parties in seven African countries:

- Boko Haram in Nigeria
- Al-Shabaab in Somalia

Chapter 10

- The Lord's Resistance Army, which is active in central African states such as the CAR, DRC, and South Sudan
- Various rebel groups in the DRC, South Sudan, Sudan, and Mali
- The ex-Seleka and anti-Balaka in the CAR
- Government forces from the DRC, Somalia, South Sudan, and Sudan.

Chad, a previous offender, was delisted from the report after it complied with all the measures set out in its action plan to end the recruitment and use of children.

The report stated that the DRC, Somalia and South Sudan had signed or recommitted to action plans to end violations against children. Sudan alone had yet to sign an action plan.

Child Soldiers in International Law

Various legal instruments have been developed over time to protect children in armed conflict. The 1977 additional protocols to the 1949 Geneva Conventions set the minimum age for recruitment and use of child soldiers in international and internal armed conflict at 15 years.

Similarly, the Convention on the Rights of the Child, which entered into force in 1990, set 15 as the minimum age for recruitment and participation in armed conflict, putting the onus on states to prevent those under 15 from being recruited into armed forces or taking direct part in hostilities.

The Convention on the Rights of the Child Optional Protocol on Children in Armed Conflict, which entered into force in 2002, obliged signatories to raise the age of

Why South Sudan Matters

voluntary recruitment from that set out in the convention, and set the benchmark for compulsory recruitment by states and participation in hostilities at 18. In terms of the agreement, non-state armed groups are not allowed to recruit or use children under the age of 18.

Under the Rome Statute, which created the International Criminal Court and also entered into force in 2002, it is a war crime for states to conscript or enlist children under the age of 15 during international conflicts, or to have them actively participate in hostilities. Similarly, the conscription or enlistment of under 15s by armed groups in internal state conflicts—and their use as active participants in combat—is criminalised.

Africa Check is a non-partisan organisation that promotes accuracy in public debate and the media. Twitter@AfricaCheck and www.africacheck.org

See this report online at https://africacheck.org/factsheets/factsheet -how-many-child-soldiers-are-there-in-africa/

PART III.
EDUCATION—THE THEATRE OF HOPE

CHAPTER 11

Education *Must* Be the Priority!

AS A RESULT OF TWO CIVIL WARS spanning nearly 50 years, any infrastructure, including the education system, was destroyed. Currently, only 27 percent of the population aged 15 years and above is literate, with significant gender disparities: the literacy rate for males is 40 percent compared to 16 percent for females. According to a 2015 estimation by UNESCO (United Nations Educational, Scientific and Cultural Organization), South Sudan had the third highest rate of illiteracy of the 147 countries listed—despite the aspirations we, the people of South Sudan, have long expressed for education and opportunities for our youth.

Today, the youth are looking to education as the tool to move themselves from poverty to self-sufficiency.

In her blog titled "The Urgency of Education in South Sudan," March 9, 2015, on the USAID Website, Linda Etim wrote:

> When I visited South Sudan in January, citizens pointed to education as a critical investment in the country's future, even in the midst of violence. A 2013 public opinion poll found 68 percent of those surveyed across South Sudan weren't satisfied with their government's performance in providing education.
>
> Yet the South Sudanese people's hopes for greater investment in and protection of their children's education are undermined by poor investments and continuing crises. Thirty-five percent of teachers in South Sudan have only a primary level of education. And while South Sudan's Ministry of Education recently reopened five teacher training institutes, officially 42 percent of the national budget goes to military and security sector costs.
>
> . . . Less than half of school-aged children in South Sudan were enrolled in school before the conflict erupted in December 2013. Since then, more than 2 million South Sudanese have been displaced by conflict, and some 400,000 students have dropped out of school. An estimated 70 percent of schools in the most conflict-affected states (Jonglei, Upper Nile, and Unity) were closed as of November 2014, and some 89 schools are currently occupied by fighting forces or internally displaced persons.
>
> . . . South Sudan will not be able to reach its potential

Chapter 11

until the country's leaders end the conflict and commit to ensuring that their nation's children have the opportunity to learn, protected from this senseless violence. https://blog.usaid.gov/2015/03/the-urgency-of-education-in -south-sudan/

Abraham Kur Achiek has firsthand knowledge of the above statement. As one of the "Lost Boys of Sudan," Abraham Kur Achiek was only 10 or 11 when he was separated from his family, and by the time he was a teenager, he was serving in the Sudan People's Liberation Army (SPLA), the rebel group that fought Sudan's Government for more than 20 years. Today, he is in his thirties and working as a Child Protection Officer for UNICEF in South Sudan.

Looking back, Mr. Achiek said the atrocities he witnessed as a young rebel soldier haunt him to this day. Even so, he credits the SPLA with giving him an education, however imperfect it may have been.

"Although the education was not of quality, I can tell you I'm proud and able to talk to you today because of the small education that I had with the SPLA." He said that it opened his eyes, and gave him an opportunity to continue looking for more education.

After escaping from the SPLA in 1994 and making it to the Kenyan border, Mr. Achiek was placed in a refugee camp, where he says education was his only hope. Learning gave him the motivation to persist with his studies.

"I did not know anybody, anywhere. So the only hope was that if I could continue with this refugee education and gain some knowledge, at least I could make some changes in my life."

Why South Sudan Matters

The SPLA and the Government of Sudan signed a Comprehensive Peace Agreement in 2005. Nonetheless, the military recruitment of children continues throughout the region. Mr. Achiek now uses his unique insight to demobilize children and prevent them from becoming associated with armed forces.

"I am able to understand them better than anyone," he says of the boys he has helped to demobilise. "I tell them to come with me, to go to school. Otherwise you will miss your childhood, you will kill, or be killed."

http://www.UNICEF.org/infobycountry/sudan_52880.html

http://www.independent.co.uk/voices/comment/the-lost-boys-of-sudans-civil-war-8434258.html

Hope for Humanity completed the construction of a secondary school in the village of Atiaba, Southern Sudan in 2007. It was only the *22nd high school to serve the over 1.5 million children.* A mere 7 percent of South Sudanese teachers at that time had any formal teacher training.

As of a 2013 report from USAID, overall in South Sudan only about half of teachers have professional qualifications and a third have only a primary school education. A quarter of those teaching students are volunteers.

According to UNESCO's 2011 Education for All Global Monitoring Report on South Sudan, "South Sudan has some of the world's worst indicators for education. Around 1 million children—half of the primary school age population—are out of school. The primary net enrollment rate is second to the bottom in world rankings, with a net enrollment rate for girls at just 37 percent. In a country with a population the

Chapter 11

size of Sweden, fewer than 400 girls make it to the last grade of secondary school. There are desperate shortages of classrooms and books—and just one qualified teacher for every 117 students."

https://blog.usaid.gov/2013/09/south-sudan-educators-acquire
-skills-to-teach-nation/

CHAPTER 12

A Sense of Urgency

THE FOLLOWING SOUTH SUDAN EDUCATION CLUSTER article best conveys the urgency for education in South Sudan:

EDUCATION CANNOT WAIT IN SOUTH SUDAN
Education Is Critical in Averting the Loss of Another Generation

Since the current crisis began in December 2013:

- 1,188 schools in the 3 most affected States (Jonglei, Unity, Upper Nile) have closed.

- Nearly half a million children and adolescents need education interventions due to the current crisis.

- Over 9,000 children have been recruited into armed forces and groups since January 2014.

- More than 90 schools in the country are occupied by fighting forces and internally displaced people.

- Lack of education is a push factor for people to leave South Sudan to neighbouring countries so their children can continue to go to school.

- South Sudan already has poor education indicators: 75 percent of the population is illiterate, 60 percent is aged under 18.

Chapter 12

Why promote education during an emergency?

- Education is life saving and life sustaining, providing psychosocial support, strengthening survival skills and coping mechanisms.
- Education is a community priority during emergencies in South Sudan.
- Education is valued by parents as a means for protection; providing safe spaces for children and adolescents protects them from dangers and exploitation.
- Education is critical for developmental needs of children and adolescents.
- Education restores schools as zones of peace and learning.
- Education is a fundamental right.

What happens next if education is not prioritised?

In 3 months [report written in 2014] . . .

- 70 percent of current emergency education in the most conflict-affected areas will stop (Unity, Upper Nile, and Jonglei States).
- Education partners will no longer be able to pay teachers' and facilitators' allowances.
- Education activities will stop. Close to half a million previously enrolled children and adolescents are out of school, and are at increased risk of engaging in negative coping strategies, recruitment into armed groups, child labor, Gender Based Violence (GBV), and violence in cramped living conditions in IDP [Internally Displaced Person] sites.
- The occupation of schools by armed groups continues and escalates; some schools are destroyed.

139

- Lifesaving messages on cholera, mine awareness, GBV, and HIV/AIDS in IDP sites may no longer reach children, adolescents, and their families.
- The longer the delay the more risk of losing another generation.

In 6 months . . .

- Essential basic learning materials run out for lack of funds.
- Supplies run out in the hardest to reach communities.
- Children miss a full academic school year. Many of them will never return to school, leading to another generation of citizens who grow up in South Sudan without an education.
- Unpaid teachers seek alternative employment, further depleting the education workforce.

In 12 months . . .

- Schools fall into disrepair and are used for other purposes; a severe shortage of teachers, even for the few schools that are open.
- More textbooks are damaged and destroyed, representing a loss of the $5 million investment in their printing and distribution in 2013.
- Dramatic increase in dropout numbers, leading to an increase in early marriage and child labor.
- Families continue to leave the country in order to access quality education for their children, straining neighbouring countries' resources.

Chapter 12

Education is a peace dividend. Hundreds of thousands of South Sudanese boys and girls continue to miss the opportunity to gain an education, something their parents had great hopes for. Since the signing of the Comprehensive Peace Agreement in 2005, funding for education has lagged behind other sectors, with educational needs increasing in South Sudan's ever recurrent conflicts.

"The other services are good but short lived . . . with education, the children will capture it and hold it forever. Human beings don't survive on just food." (Community Leader, Juba IDP camp)

"I want to be literate." (Schoolgirl, aged 12, on why she is attending the emergency education school in an IDP site in Juba)

"We have already forgotten what we learned in school because it has been so long. We are ready to go back." (Schoolboy, aged 12)

http://www.protectingeducation.org/sites/default/files/documents/education_cannot_wait_in_south_sudan_2014.pdf

PART IV.
SURVIVING THE WAR

CHAPTER 13

Higher Education— No Bed of Roses

I CAN'T SAY THAT LIFE IN KENYA WAS SMOOTH, but when I started pursuing a higher level of education, it gave me the opportunity to broaden my horizons. I learned to be tolerant of other people's opinions and ideas . . . and never fight. Before, there was a fight if I even heard an offensive word. We grew up being defensive to anything that touched our surroundings. The opportunity of education was to me another journey, but this time with no bloodshed. Rather, I had to struggle to remember everything I was being taught because it wasn't *my* history—it was the history of my neighbouring countries. I was tested on my knowledge of their

Chapter 13

countries; my background was lost. The heroes I knew about as I grew up were less important. I was judged by my knowledge of the Kenyan colonial period.

Whenever a teacher asked us to think of a story to write, my colleagues would always write about the first president of Kenya, Mzee Jomo Kenyatta, and the rest of the heroes. I would always write about a Sudanese hero, Sultan Awan Anei, and would be given a score of three out of ten. The teacher didn't know the importance of Sultan Awan Anei and how he saved the lives of the people. He fought in the clan wars—northern Sudan versus southern Sudan. He fought the Arabs and won all his battles. The people of South Sudan could have been Muslims, but thanks to him, they are Christians. (The generations that followed have now seen the independence of South Sudan.) Christianity was introduced to the southern Sudanese by the British during the colonial period that began in the 1800s. The southern Sudanese were animists, but the Christian missionaries were accepted when the Arabs of Northern Sudan tried to force Muslim education on them.

Learning to adapt was a struggle, yet necessary if I were to pass my exams. I had grasped the importance of education as a means to have a future better than my past, so nothing could stand in the way of that—not even my own attitude. So, I started writing about Kenyan historical heroes, and I did well. I was able to attend the best high school in the country. My adapting helped me succeed, and soon I finished my studies at Laiser Hill Academy high school.

My grades took me to the University of Nairobi, the number one university in Kenya, and third best in Africa. It was there that I realised I had to start giving back to the community. My career choice must reflect what my community in South Sudan needed. I came from a civil war society, and I was a child soldier in that war. Our country was full of hate and killed those who did not have the same ideas as ours. A soldier without political ideology was considered a criminal, so we children, who were only looking for survival, were "criminals." However, we never robbed, nor did we kill for pleasure.

In university, I first chose law, but I reconsidered because it was going to take a long time, and I had been away from my parents for many years. Instead I chose criminology and social order as a diploma, while I did political science, sociology and armed conflict, and peace study as a degree course. My choice was influenced by the fact that our country needed good leadership. Bad leadership had misled most African countries even when those countries are given a chance to lead themselves. I knew that choice of study would allow me to influence the citizens in choosing the right leadership for our country. It would also enable me to proclaim peace among the young generation, to understand the needs of the people, and to support those who do not know their rights.

My university life was fun, especially compared with my previous work experience, life experience, war experience—whatever one would call it—but that experience taught me a lot. It taught me to appreciate whatever life offers; and to appreciate simple things such as people who look at me and smile instead of the tough, scary faces I had seen in the past—those who only knew killing. How I survived the war is a miracle. I lost close friends—boys and girls my age who grew up as I did, on our own, trying to stay alive. We would fall in an ambush, and in less than ten minutes, many of them

Chapter 13

had died. Even though so many of our friends and relatives are gone, God has brought together those of us who are left to make a country. I first knew of God when I was in Ethiopia—when life had no meaning for me and there was no one I could turn to. I was introduced to God and saw Him as the best way to change that horrible time of my life into a blessing. My life changed . . . I changed, and I follow God to this day.

My free time in University was spent envisaging the chances God had given me in life—times when I saw death and angels saved me. I have no other explanation. I survived not because I was tough, but because God saved me. I look back at how we used to study under trees and how we would sometimes sleep the whole day because we had no food. I do not want that history to be lost. Hope was the only *food* that kept us alive—not big dreams for the future, just that there would be food for that day and the next. Such visions would come to my mind, and then I would pray to God and thank him for giving me a purpose in life. God has always been good to me and to my people. I felt that I must be a good servant and example for others to follow God—the One who cares for us, loves us, and protects us from danger.

I saw movies of Rambo, Commando, Chuck Norris, Jackie Chan, Will Smith, Taylor Terry, Chris Tucker, all those movie actors in Hollywood. I could relate and see myself as a survivor like them. The movie world was real to me, as I saw depicted on the screen my own survival in a war-torn country. I knew I had something in common with Chris Tucker and all the blacks and whites who live in ghettos in America. Death is close to them. I thought if God could bring me through 21 years of civil war, he had a purpose for my life.

This encouraged me daily to work hard and focus on my education.

I was a youth leader as well as a community leader while I was in Nairobi. In my free time after lectures at the University, I decided to write down my thoughts about the civil war events and the survival of my friends, family, and relatives. The struggle of my people of South Sudan in search of peace and independence has never ended. I wanted to write about how the children miss an education in life, how they become the victims of the adult ideology, suffering under a struggle they know nothing about, and how mothers have to be separated from their children.

I wrote about the civil war, and how it affected me and my generation and all those who were born during the war. As a child I felt it was a mistake to be born during a war; why couldn't the parents wait until the war was over before having children? My young mind could not understand. It wasn't long before my writing turned into a book.

At first I doubted my English; I knew what I wanted to say, but my English was poor. As my friends read the developing manuscript and encouraged me, I became more confident. I realized that English is a language, not a tool to measure my intelligence. As long as my ideas made sense, I knew that one day I would find someone who could shape my work so the world would know what we have suffered.

I titled my first book *The Theatre of Hope*. I focused on education in South Sudan and how war has affected it. It was largely autobiographical. I knew that in order to capture the reality of our society, it had to be my story.

I then began raising funds to publish my book and launch it. It was a challenge, as no one believed in my work. For

Chapter 13

some it was jealousy, while for others it was partly the African belief that young people cannot write a book; only old people can write.

When I told my uncle Tong Deng about my book, he was very excited and was willing to support me in any way he could. He had worked with the United Nations since 1993, and was working as a Minister for Health in Northern Bahr el Ghazal where my dad was a Governor.

He was the only one who believed in my work. He supported me, encouraged me, and in no time I was launching my book at Serena Hotel, Nairobi, Kenya, on March 13, 2013, attended by Kenyan Minister of Education, Professor Sam Ongeri. I received a nice compliment from him, and then my name was all over the media. I got e-mails, phone calls, texts and messages through my social media from as far away as America, Australia, and the UK, as well as from the South Sudanese society in diaspora and back home.

I imagined a movie made in South Sudan, based on the book, that would show all we had been through—how we survived war attacks while others were shot and died right in front of us. A movie would make our horror more of a reality for those who saw it on the screen. I could see Will Smith, Rambo, Commando, Chris Tucker, Chuck Norris, Jackie Chan and all the Hollywood actors and actresses like Angelina Jolie, Emma Stone, Olivia Wilde, Marion Cotillard, Megan Fox and Natalie Portman. I saw them in their roles as survivors of hardship, just as we had been for the past two decades.

Although there were many positive elements to my writing the book, the most amazing was hearing from my mother after our thirteen-year separation with absolutely no contact

147

with each other. I kept heart and never stopped hoping that she was alive. In my country, children were not given news of death because it was thought to demoralize them. The circumstances when I last saw her were dire. The drought had just begun, all of the food stores had been burned by the government forces and they had almost overrun the rebellion.

Due to the excellent coverage of the book, she learned where I was. She was able to access a satellite phone from a UN worker and she called me. With a great deal of excitement in her voice she said, "My son, I heard you wrote a book, is it true?"

"Yes, Mum," I said.

"In which language?" She asked me this with a smile in her voice. If only someone could have taken a picture of her so I could see her face. I have never heard my mother so happy.

"Of course I didn't use Dinka language, Mum. It's in English."

All she could do was laugh. And then she said, "Nying' gilizi you wrote the book." Meaning, you wrote the book in the English language. "Okay my son, God bless you my son. Let me ask you, have you written all the suffering we the people of South Sudan have gone through?" She hesitated, waiting for the answer.

"Mum, I have written everything." I wanted to cut her questions short in order to get a chance to hear all about what had happened to her and how people were doing at home. It had been so long since I had heard her voice.

"My son, I hope you wrote about all the tree leaves we ate, all the days without food, how we suffered under the religion that was forced on us, how we walked from Awiel East State

Chapter 13

to Ethiopia by foot." She said many things I don't know how to translate to English, but I told her I had written everything.

I knew this would be the talk of the small town we come from. Now the community would know that they sent out a son who would come back and help them in the near future.

I knew that everything I had done, everything I had suffered, was for the sake of my people, my mother, the orphans, and the fallen heroes of South Sudan.

CHAPTER 14
Home to South Sudan

WHEN I FINISHED UNIVERSITY, it was the beginning of a new chapter in my life—a chapter that would be the most challenging of all. Could I show the people who sacrificed so I could go to school that I would deliver my services to the community?

I first returned to my hometown of Warawar, and then to Juba, the capital of South Sudan. Juba, where the sun is lower, just above the trees—hot as hell, but I don't know hell, so it could be hotter than hell—Juba, divided by the longest river in the world, the River Nile.

When I returned to South Sudan, the rebels were also coming back. The competition for jobs was high between those with guns and those with pens—the freedom fighters who had held on to their guns and we scholars who dropped our guns at the age of fifteen in search of education in the refugee camps of neighbouring countries.

While in University, my food was provided for me, but now I had to search for kombo and kisira, our local food. I had no home, and had to rely on my cousin, Santino Muong, for accommodations. He had cleared university a year ahead of me and had a job.

As I walked around the city in the hot sun, I could see

150

Chapter 14

orphans and widows struggling to subsist with no papers to support their qualifications for jobs. This inspired me to write about the children of the freedom fighters. Writing was a bit easier this time; I knew all the challenges I was going to face. The search for a job was a nightmare. I had many sleepless nights not only worrying about a job, but thinking about how I could make a positive impact on our society in my own way. I registered a community-based organization called "CHILD TO CHILD EDUCATION." It advocated for the rights of the children of the forgotten freedom fighters. I became an icon of children's rights, and was consulted by most of the youth if anything was to be done in the society or among the communities.

In my free time, I assisted in lecturing at the Christian University in Juba. I was paid five dollars per hour for a three-hour lecture, twice a week. Although I went mainly to share my knowledge with my own generation, I really did need money.

Whenever I went back to Warawar, I taught in a local primary school to give back to the community. This time I did it for no payment. I was committed to do whatever I could for my people.

When the new government was formed and President Salva Kiir appointed new governors, the youth wrote a letter to the president, sent a copy to the newly appointed governor, and took another copy to the office of the ruling party requesting Garang Malong Awan as a minister in the new, yet to be formed, ministerial. This was the beginning of my political career.

What the youth saw in me was not about my father being

a freedom fighter, nor was it about my background; it was about my potential, my hard work, my focus, and what I had achieved thus far. Having written about the impact of war on education, having remembered the children of the forgotten freedom fighters, and continually writing articles that concerned the innocent people of South Sudan, they saw in me someone whom they wanted to be their leader, and that I should represent them in the government as a Minister for Youth, Culture and Sport. They did their best to make the public believe in my potential and in me.

At the time, South Sudan still had only ten states. After a few months of lobbying, it was announced on the National Television that I was the newly appointed Minister of Youth, Culture and Sport in our state, Awiel East. Although I am the second son of my father, and in my culture the firstborn takes first place or any first opportunity in life, in this case it was different. The youth saw potential for cooperation that could last forever, a union that could help put our nation back together. They knew that I am a man who will not forget those who are in need—especially the youth and women—and that I would be a good representative for both.

Many people were happy over my appointment. The time had come for the youth. My appointment meant that more of our country's youth would come to power, and there would be gentle change.

I spent my youth running for my life, trying to save myself from an enemy I never wronged—an enemy that hated me for my colour, my religion, my geographical region. I couldn't understand it, but even at a very young age I knew that the best thing I could do would be to stay alive for the next generation to come. Those of us who survived growing

Chapter 14

up in civil war and its aftermath did not have much of an opportunity to think about our capacity, our ability, our talent—we had to search for our own identity. We are the future of our country. I have a saying, "If they don't want to save it but wish to destroy it, we will save it and lead it."

Our society has been broken, but we thank God that the government is doing its best to provide for its people. As I am writing this last chapter, I have received word that I was chosen as the new Minister for Education and Child Welfare in Awiel East State.

I know that none of the amazing things that have happened to me would have been possible without my having had the opportunity for an education. I am so very thankful. It is my passion that there will be thousands coming behind me who will have this same opportunity. There will then be a new, wonderful chapter in our great nation of South Sudan.

A Debt of Gratitude

I COULD NOT FINISH THIS BOOK without commending those who have played such an important part in the independence of my beloved country of South Sudan. My heartfelt thanks and appreciation to the following:

~ Our neighbouring countries that stood with us, offering refuge, solace and even education when we had nowhere to go—Ethiopia, Kenya, Uganda, we thank you. I appreciate all the presidents and heads of state of those countries as well as other African countries—Angola, Egypt, Eritrea, South Africa, Zimbabwe. We know that we did not achieve this independence alone, nor will we be able to develop this nation alone. It will take all of us standing together to make a bright future for our people.

~ Israel—the relations between South Sudan and the State of Israel began in the late 1960s when visiting Israel was a punishable offense in Sudan; thus, Southerners maintained ties with Israel at a great personal risk. The bilateral ties between the state of Israel and the Republic of South Sudan are strong to this day.

The American Jewish Committee's Africa Institute came to South Sudan in 2008 with their intention to support South

A Debt of Gratitude

Sudan. They met with government officials and learned of ways in which the diaspora in Israel might be involved in the state-building efforts in preparation for independence.

Israel was the first country that recognized South Sudan as an independent state on July 10, 2011, a day after the flag was raised. This was followed by South Sudan's announcement on July 15 of its intention to have full diplomatic relations with Israel. Thirteen days later Israel announced their having established full diplomatic relations with South Sudan.

The economic support Israel has given South Sudan has been vital, and our people are grateful—not only for their financial assistance, but for always believing in us.

~ Former U.S. President George W. Bush and his administration, the nation of Norway, the United Nations and other non-government organizations—we thank you for all your support and love for our nation. Our people will always be grateful for your courage to stand with us when all seemed hopeless.

Through former President George W. Bush, the whole world came to understand that our struggle was real. His words were clear and helped guide us to be the independent nation we have long desired—one of peace, love, unity, one with the right to religion, the right to live anywhere in the country we choose, the right to education, and most important, the right to life. The South Sudanese people will always be grateful to former President George W. Bush and all those who worked with him, such as former U.S. Secretary of State Condoleezza Rice. There are those who are alive in South Sudan today due to the intervention of America.

On July 9, 2011, the diverse citizens of South Sudan gathered at the square to celebrate the independent nation of South Sudan. The flag of South Sudan was flying high—a sign of unity and the fruit of our long struggle. Thanks were given accordingly; former President George W. Bush and Condoleezza Rice (called "Mother" with great respect by the locals for her outstanding support of our country) among others are so much appreciated. Young men and women started naming themselves Bush Chol while others were called Condoleezza Aluat. Those expecting babies planned on using the names of great leaders who had made such a change in their lives—from years of unrelenting conflict; from hiding in the forest to living openly in their towns. Moreover, they wished their children to be like these leaders. Names like Unity, Independence, Peace, Separation, and Freedom were also used as names for the children, companies, and hotels in South Sudan.

To all those mentioned in this last part of the book who have always stood with us, it must seem that our thanks have been a long time coming. In our struggle to attain these goals, nations and individuals have stood by our side to encourage us with moral and humanitarian support, and that will never be forgotten. Our struggle is not over. We have a new country to develop, but together we can do this. Thank you.

I now offer my undying gratitude to a very special group of people—the Freedom Fighters of South Sudan. These soldiers, mothers, and fathers had a vision for our country—a vision that our grandfathers and grandmothers had before

A Debt of Gratitude

them. They knew where they came from; they knew the history of the Cush, the black people of Sudan, the people found in the upper Nile region: people recognized by the Bible in all seven verses of Isaiah 18.

Our fathers and mothers had the same vision and believed in our independent country. They went together to the frontlines and into the bush. When soldiers went to war, mothers went with them to provide them with water, food, and bullets at the front line. Their presence helped the leadership keep their focus. Sometimes children were left in frightening circumstances with only their mothers to care for them. Independence was a collective effort of those on the front line and those taking care of the next generation at home.

Most important, we give our thanks to the SPLA (Sudan People's Liberation Army) soldiers and commanders, and SPLM (Sudan People's Liberation Movement) leadership for their firm stand to bring our people independence.

Our fathers and mothers of SPLA have shown us love, care and protection throughout the struggle. When we, the African people, were discriminated against by the intruders who looked at our skin or our religion and thought us unworthy, our grandfathers and grandmothers stood, took up arms, and defended the territory of the Cush people . . . the people along the Nile Valley . . . the black of Sudan . . . the present day people of South Sudan. They knew the consequences, but even so, their vision was carried on from generation to generation.

Our fathers, brothers, sisters, and mothers fought for this nation. They went to war knowing they were going to die, yet they chose death to bring peace and freedom of religion to the people of South Sudan.

Without the leadership of the SPLA/M, the vison would have been lost. Thanks to the focus and well-coordinated effort by commanders from different communities—those who led the Bahr el Ghazal region of Awiel, in Wau, Kuajok, Rumbek,the Equatoria region, and those in the Upper Nile region, we are now the independent nation of South Sudan.

We appreciate our sovereign President of the Republic of South Sudan, Salva Kiir Mayardit; all the leaders of the nation; our Chief of General Staff of the Armed Forces; our soldiers; our ministers and members of parliament; our sultans and all the leaders of the nation for their contribution to our freedom. Thank you.

BOOK THREE

Patriotism—South Sudan, My Country

INTRODUCTION

The South Sudan spirit is upon the young and the leaders who serve this nation with love and sacrifice for the freedom of this nation.

Patriotism, according to the *Macmillan Dictionary*, is "strong feelings of love, respect and duty toward your country . . . Community and the feeling of belonging to a community." When a nation needs to prosper, the people should practice the spirit of patriotism.

In a nation that practices patriotism, vices such as corruption, tribalism, nepotism, and greed do not exist.

Those who practice tribalism do not embrace love and unity; those who practice corruption misuse public resources for their own personal gain. The greedy want everything for themselves, e.g., land grabbing. Nepotism is the use of an individual's office, power, and influence to favour their relatives or tribesmen and women with jobs.

Corruption is the act of stealing, accepting bribes, or giving bribes in order to receive something in return. It is common among the police and those who hold public office. It can occur anytime, anywhere.

A patriotic person is proud of his or her country's culture and history, and should embrace them in order to allow their continuity.

A patriotic person loves and supports the development of the country, much like the business owners and musicians of South Sudan, and defends his country, such as our freedom fighters have done.

How did our freedom fighters display their patriotism to South Sudan?

Patriotism—South Sudan, My Country

Our freedom fighters display their patriotism by:

- Writing the law that will guide the people of South Sudan

- Respecting the national flag

- Fighting corruption, tribalism, and nepotism in all of South Sudan

- Honoring the national anthem, respecting those who are in authority, and protecting and promoting the rights of others

What could the people of South Sudan do at this time in addition to that list?

- We should conserve our national resources, and strive to keep the environment clean. We should participate in national elections and community development services.

- We should all pay taxes.

- We should serve our country with diligence, love, and honour.

- National days should be respected by all of us.

The ten destructive "ideals" of South Sudan's evil spirits are:

1. Tribalism	6. Inequality
2. Injustice	7. Corruption
3. Greed	8. Dishonesty
4. Nepotism	9. Laziness
5. Murder	10. Jealousy

Our flag has six distinguishing colours:

- **White** for peace attained after many years of the liberation struggle

- **Black** for black African skin

- **Blue** for the waters of the Nile River—a source of life for South Sudan

- **Yellow** for unity of the states of South Sudan

- **Red** for blood that was shed by the martyrs of the liberation struggle

- **Green** for South Sudan's natural resources and verdant land

OUR LANGUAGE

Although we are diversified, our official language unites us as one people. Our official language is English.

OUR RESOURCES

Our strength is in our resources.

- The effective use of our human resource, manpower, is the beginning of patriotism.

- Our fertile land can be used for agriculture.

- Oil is a major resource of South Sudan; gold follows.

Patriotism—South Sudan, My Country

OUR NATIONAL ANTHEM

Oh God!

We praise and glorify You
For Your grace on South Sudan,
The land of great abundance
Uphold us united in peace and harmony.

Oh motherland!
We rise raising flag with the guiding star
And sing songs of freedom with joy;
For justice, liberty and prosperity
Shall forever more reign.

Oh great patriots!
Let us stand up in silence and respect,
Saluting our martyrs whose blood
Cemented our national foundation,
We vow to protect our nation.
Oh God, bless South Sudan!

Acknowledgments

To my father, Paul Malong Awan, and my mother, Achol Kuel Athian, who ensured that I realize my academic dream. I am what I am today because of their relentless support and belief in me.

Ellen Ratner is a true friend of South Sudan. She has worked tirelessly to bring hope, health, and education to my country. Through her encouragement and influence I was convinced that the message of South Sudan needed to extend beyond our own borders.

My editor, Shari Johnson, caught my vision and passion for South Sudan and "translated" my African culture into terms the rest of the world could understand.

About the Author

Honorable Garang Malong Awan is a lifelong resident of his beloved South Sudan. After a sporadic, sometimes inadequate early education, he graduated from the University of Nairobi in Kenya, Africa. His focus of degree study included Political Science, Sociology, Armed Conflict, and Peace Studies with a diploma in Criminology and Social Order, and a concurrent certificate in Public Relations.

His natural leadership ability and his passion for improving the educational system in South Sudan led to his appointment and success as Minister of Education and Social Child Welfare. He states that, because of the hardships he endured as a child, "I had a chance to help others, as I knew what they were suffering from my own experience."

He now serves as Minister of Agriculture and Forestry in Aweil East State, noted for its farming and cattle, which helps feed others in the region with milk and meat.

About his book he says, "My life's struggle has been put to rest with pen and paper, not with guns and bullets."